Alice, Let's Eat

Alice, Let's Eat

FURTHER ADVENTURES OF A HAPPY EATER

Calvin Trillin

RANDOM HOUSE/NEW YORK

Library of Congress Cataloging in Publication Data
Trillin, Calvin.
Alice, let's eat.
1. Dinners and dining. I. Title.
TX737.T74   641'.013   77–90295
ISBN 0–394–42500–6
Portions of Chapters 3, 4, 7, 10, 11 and 14 originally appeared, in
somewhat different form, in The New Yorker, Copyright © 1973,
1976 and 1977 by Calvin Trillin. Portions of other chapters originally
appeared, in different form, in Travel & Leisure (Chapters 1, 2, 5
and 13), Copyright © 1975, 1977 and 1978 by Calvin Trillin;
Esquire (Chapters 5 and 12), Copyright © 1976 by Calvin Trillin;
TWA Ambassador (Chapter 6), Copyright © 1974 by Calvin Trillin;
and The Atlantic Monthly (Chapter 15), Copyright © 1978
by Calvin Trillin.

Manufactured in the United States of America

2 4 6 8 9 7 5 3

First Edition

To Alice, of course

Contents

Alice, Let's Eat

I

Alice

Now that it's fashionable to reveal intimate details of married life, I can state publicly that my wife, Alice, has a weird predilection for limiting our family to three meals a day. I also might as well admit that the most serious threat to our marriage came in 1975, when Alice mentioned my weight just as I was about to sit down to dinner at a New Orleans restaurant named Chez Helène. I hardly need add that Chez Helène is one of my favorite restaurants in New Orleans; we do not have the sort of marriage that could come to grief over ordinary food.

Without wanting to be legalistic, I should mention that Alice brought up the weight issue during a long-distance telephone call—breaking whatever federal regulations there are against Interstate Appetite Impairment. Like many people who travel a lot on business, I'm in the habit of calling home every evening to share the little victories and defeats of the day—the triumph, for instance, of happening upon a superior tamale stand in a town I thought had long before been completely carved into spheres of influence by McDonald's and Burger King, or the misery of being escorted by some local booster past the unmistakable aroma of genuine hickory-wood barbecuing into La Maison de la Casa House, whose notion of "Continental cuisine" seems to have been derived in some arcane way from the Continental-Trailways bus company. Having found myself on business in New Orleans—or, as it is sometimes expressed around my office, having found it my business to find business in New Orleans—I was about to settle into Chez Helène for a long evening. First, of course, I telephoned Alice in New York. I assumed it would give her great pleasure to hear that her husband was about to have enough sweet potatoes and fried oysters to make him as happy as he could manage to be outside her presence. Scholars of the art have often mentioned Chez Helène as an example of what happens when Creole blends with Soul— so that a bowl of greens comes out tasting of spices that the average greens-maker in Georgia or Alabama probably associates with papists or the Devil himself.

"I'm about to have dinner at Chez Helène," I said.

"Dr. Seligmann just told me today that you weighed a hundred and eighty pounds when you were in his office last week," Alice said. "That's terrible!"

"There must be something wrong with this connection," I said. "I could swear I just told you that I was about to have dinner at Chez Helène."

"You're going to have to go on a diet. This is serious."

It occurred to me that a man telephoning his wife from a soul-food restaurant could, on the excuse of trying to provide some authentic atmosphere, say something like "Watch yo' mouth, woman!" Instead, I said, "I think there might be a better time to talk about this, Alice." Toward the end of the second or third term of the Caroline Kennedy Administration was the sort of time I had in mind.

"Well, we can talk about it when you get home," Alice said. "Have a nice dinner."

I did. It is a measure of my devotion to Alice that I forgave her, even though my second order of fried chicken was ruined by the realization that I had forgotten to tell her I had actually weighed only a hundred and sixty-six pounds. I always allow fourteen pounds for clothes.

I must say that Alice tempers her rigidity on the meals-per-day issue by having a broad view of what constitutes an hors d'oeuvre. That is not, of course, her only strong point. She is tenacious, for instance—having persisted for five or six summers in attempting to wheedle the recipe for the seafood chowder served at Gladee's Canteen, in Hirtle's Beach, Nova Scotia, out of the management. She is imaginative—a person who can turn a bucketful of clams into, on successive evenings, steamed clams, clam fritters, clams in white wine sauce, and a sort of clam billi-bi. I can testify to her restraint: on the Christmas I presented her with a Cuisinart food processor, not having realized that what she really wanted was a briefcase, she thanked me politely, the way an exceedingly courteous person might thank a process server for a subpoena. ("Well," I finally said. "I thought it might be good for mulching the Christmas tree.") She is generous—the sort of wife who would share even the tiniest order of, say, crawfish bisque with her husband, particularly if he had tears in his eyes when he asked. Alice has a lot of nice qualities, but when someone tells me, as someone often does, how fortunate I am to have her as my wife, I generally say, "Yes, she does have a broad view of what constitutes an hors d'oeuvre."

I don't mean that her views on this matter are as broad as the views held by our friend Fats Goldberg, the New York pizza baron and reformed blimp, who, in reporting on the semiannual eating binges in Kansas City he still allows himself, often begins sentences with phrases like "Then on the way to lunch I stopped at Kresge's for a chili dog." A Kresge chili dog, it seems to me, reflects a view of hors d'oeuvres that has strayed from broad to excessive. (It also reflects the fact that Fats Goldberg in binge gear will eat almost anything but green vegetables.) What I mean is that if we happen to be driving through Maine on our way to Nova Scotia, where we live in the summer, Alice does not object when, ten miles from the lobster restaurant where we plan to stop for dinner, I screech to a halt in front of a place that has the look of a spectacular fried-clam stand. "It'll make a nice hors d'oeuvre," she says.

While I'm speaking in Alice's defense, I should also say that I consider her failure with the children half my own: no one person could be responsible for engendering in two innocent little girls a preference for frozen fish sticks over fish. In fact, in Nova Scotia I have seen Alice take a halibut that was on a fishing boat an hour before, sprinkle it ever so slightly with some home-ground flour, fry it for a few seconds until it is covered with a batter whose lightness challenges the batter on a Gladee's fishball, cut it into sticklike slices, and present it to her very own little girls—only to have them pick at it for a few minutes and gaze longingly toward the freezer.

Oddly enough, both of our girls have shown, in quick, maddening flashes, indications of having been born with their taste buds intact. Once, while we were visiting my mother in Kansas City, Abigail, our older daughter, looked up at me during breakfast and said, "Daddy, how come in Kansas City the bagels just taste like round bread?" Her father's daughter, I allowed myself to hope—a connoisseur of bagels before she's five. By age nine she'll probably be able to identify any bialy she eats by borough of origin; she'll pick up some change after school working at Russ & Daughters Appetizer Store as a whitefish taster. On trips to Kansas City, her proud father's hometown, she'll appear as a child prodigy on the stage of the concert hall, lecturing on the varieties of the local barbecue sauce. Not so. At nine, offered anything that does not have the familiarity of white chicken or hamburger or Cheerios, she declines with a "No, thank you" painful in its elaborate politeness. This is the daughter who, at the age of four, reacted to a particularly satisfying dish of chocolate ice cream by saying, "My tongue is smiling." How quickly for parents do the disappointments come.

Abigail's younger sister, Sarah, has a palate so unadventurous that she refuses to mix peanut butter with jelly. I have often told her that I hope she chooses a college rather close to home—New York University, perhaps, which is in Greenwich Village, just a few blocks from where we live—so that when I show up every morning to cut the crusts off her toast I won't require a sleepover. For a couple of years, Sarah refused to enter a Chinese restaurant unless she was carrying a bagel in reserve. "Just in case," she often explained. More than once, Alice and Abigail and I, all having forgotten Sarah's special requirements, started to leave for a family dinner in Chinatown only to hear a small, insistent voice cry, "My bagel! My bagel!"

One night, in a Chinese restaurant, Sarah became a fancier of roast squab. We were at the Phoenix Gardens, a place in Chinatown that happens to have, in addition to excellent roast squab, a dish called Fried Fresh Milk with Crabmeat, which tastes considerably better than it sounds, and a shrimp dish that is one of the closest New York equivalents to the sort of shrimp served in some Italian restaurants in New Orleans. Just why Sarah would decide to taste roast squab still puzzles historians, since it is known that three months were required for Abigail, perhaps the only human being she completely trusts, to persuade her that chocolate ice cream was really something worth trying. Sarah herself has always treated her passion for a single exotic food-stuff as something that requires no explanation—like a mortgage officer who, being sober and cautious and responsible in every other way, sees nothing peculiar about practicing voodoo on alternate Thursdays. During lunch once in Nova Scotia, the subject of favorite foods was brought up by a friend of ours named Shelly Stevens, who is a year or two older than Abigail and is known among gourmets in Queens County mainly for being just about the only person anybody has ever heard of who eats banana peels as well as bananas. Sarah looked up from her peanut-butter sandwich—hold the jelly—and said, "Squab. Yes. Definitely squab."

It is not really Alice's fault that our girls are subject to bad influences. One morning, while I was preparing lunches for them to take to P. S. 3, I unwrapped some ham—some remarkably good Virginia ham that Alice had somehow managed to unearth in a store around the corner otherwise notable only for the number of hours each day the checkout counter clerk manages to spend doing her nails. Sarah said she didn't want any ham. It turned out that she had trouble eating a ham sandwich for lunch because a little girl with a name like Moira would always sit next to her and tell her how yucky ham was—Moira being a strict vegetarian, mung-bean and bean-sprout division.

"The people who warned us about sending our children to public school in New York were right," I said to Alice. "Now our daughter is being harassed by a mad-dog vegetarian."

Alice was opposed to my suggestion that Sarah attempt to place Moira under citizen's arrest. At the least, I thought Sarah should tell Moira that bean sprouts are the yuckiest food of all except for mung beans, and that carrot juice makes little girls pigeon-toed and bad at arithmetic. As it happens, health food does disagree with me. I tend to react to eating one of those salads with brown grass and chopped walnuts the way some people react to eating four or five fried Italian sausages. (I, on the other hand, react to eating four or five fried Italian sausages with a quiet smile.) Alice claims that what bothers me is not health food but the atmosphere of the health-food restaurants in our neighborhood—some of which seem modeled on the last days of a particularly unsuccessful commune. It's a neat theory, but it does not account for the time in Brunswick, Maine, when— during a festival whose atmosphere was absolutely splendid —I was fed something advertised as "whole foods for the multitudes" and immediately felt as if I had taken a very long journey in a very small boat. Fortunately, someone at the festival had mentioned hearing that a diner just outside of Brunswick served chili spicy enough to charbroil the

tongue, and just a small cup of it turned out to be an antidote that had me feeling chipper enough to order some
more. I had realized I was at the right diner even before I
sat down: a sign on the door said, "When you're hungry
and out of work, eat an environmentalist."

Now and then—when Alice mentions, say, the nutritional value of brown rice—I have begun to worry that she
might have fallen under the influence of the Natural Food
Fanatics or the Balanced Diet Conspiracy. Once they
learned of her fundamentalist views on Three Meals a Day,
after all, they might have figured that they had a foot in the
door. Could it be, I wonder in my most suspicious moments, that Moira's mother has been sneaking in for missionary work—waiting until I'm out of town, then clunking
over in her leather sandals from her food co-op meeting to
talk up the health-giving properties of organically grown
figs? In calmer moments I admit to myself that Alice's
awareness of, say, the unspeakable destruction wrought by
refined sugar is probably just another example of knowl-
edge she seems to have absorbed from no immediately as-
certainable source. Occasionally, for instance, we have
come home from a party and I have said, with my usual
careful choice of words, "What was that funny-looking
thing whatsername was wearing?" Then Alice—the serious
academic who teaches college students to write and explains
foreign movies to her husband, the mother of two who still
refers to those rich ladies who swoop through midtown
stores as "grownups"—tells me who designed the funny-
looking thing and how much it probably cost and which
tony boutique peddled it and why some people believe it to
be chic. At such moments I am always stunned—as if I had

idly wondered out loud about the meaning of some inscription on a ruin in Oaxaca and Alice had responded by translating fluently from the Toltec.

I admit that Moira's mother has never been spotted coming out of our house by a reliable witness. I admit that the girls do not show the vulnerability to Natural Food propaganda they might show if their own mother were part of the conspiracy. Sarah, in fact, once left a summer nursery program in Kansas City because the snacktime included salad. "They gave me salad!" she says to this day, in the tone a countess roughly handled by the customs man might say, "They searched my gown!"

All in all, I admit that Alice is, in her own way, a pretty good eater herself. The last time she failed to order dessert, for instance, was in the spring of 1965, in a Chinese restaurant that offered only canned kumquats. I have been with her in restaurants when she exulted over the purity and simplicity of the perfectly broiled fresh sea bass she had ordered, and then finished off the meal with the house specialty of toasted pound cake covered with ice cream and chocolate sauce. I suppose her only serious weakness as an eater—other than these seemingly uncontrollable attacks of moderation—is that she sometimes lets her mind wander between meals. I first began to notice this weakness when we were traveling in Italy just after we got married. ("It all shows up on the honeymoon," the wise heads used to say when the subject of marriage came up at LeRoy's Waldo Bar in Kansas City.) There we were in Italy, and Alice was devoting a good hour and a half right in the middle of the morning to inspecting a cathedral instead of helping me to comb the Michelin guide for the lunch spot most likely to stagger us with the perfection of its fettucine. I tried to explain to her that marriage is sharing—not merely sharing one's fettucine with one's husband if he is gazing at it adoringly and is obviously having second thoughts about having ordered the veal, but sharing the burden of finding the fettucine restaurant in the first place.

Since then, Alice has, as they say, grown in the marriage —and so, in another way, have I. Still, there are times when, in a foreign country, she will linger in a museum in front of some legendary piece of art as the morning grows late and I become haunted by the possibility that the restaurant I have chosen for lunch will run out of garlic sausage before we get there. "Alice!" I say on those occasions, in a stage whisper that sometimes fails to get her attention even though the museum guards turn to glare in my direction. "Alice! Alice, let's eat!"

2

Off the Beach

After Alice and I spent a week in Martinique one winter, I finally began to sympathize with those hard-driving business executives who are so jumpy on the beach that their wives spend the entire vacation telling them to relax: I was in a constant state of tension over such matters as whether I should have had the *crabes farcis* rather than the *calalou* as an appetizer. We all have our own sources of stress.

"Relax," Alice said. I was pacing the sand as usual, giving a pretty good imitation of a frenzied conglomerateur possessed by the fear that he had swallowed up a company that would prove to be indigestible.

"But I just realized that Le Gommier is particularly renowned for its *crabes farcis*," I said, referring to a small restaurant in Fort de France where we had eaten ourselves to distraction the previous day.

"But you said you loved the *calalou*," she said, soothingly.

True. I loved it. *Calalou* is a sort of puréed vegetable soup—a spicy marvel whose texture fuels my suspicion that buried somewhere in those gastronomic histories of how the French and African cultures came together in the French West Indies to create creole cooking is the information that a Waring blender was introduced in the islands in 1863. On the other hand, *crabes farcis* are stuffed crabs, and chefs on Martinique tend to use as stuffing what I suspect a crab would have chosen to stuff himself with if only he had been given the opportunity.

"And you said the *blaff d'oursins* was spectacular," she said. "I'm sure you made the right choice with the *blaff d'oursins*."

She used the tone the wife of the hard-driving conglomerateur might use to calm him down ("I'm sure it was a very nice company to have swallowed up, dear"). She was right, of course. *Blaff* is what people in Martinique call a sort of stew they make, heavy on the limes. I think I had been put off at first merely because the word *blaff* sounds so much like what Sarah says when presented with unfamiliar food. When I first saw it on the menu, I responded the way I might respond to being offered some French dish called, say, *yuque de champignons*. Then I realized that *blaff d'oursins* has a rather noble sound to it ("Suddenly, she saw him riding out of the darkness—the Count Henri-Claude Blaff d'Oursins, a fearfully handsome man who disarmed the evil Fouchard with a casual flip of his sword.") *Oursins* are sea urchins, and, while eating the version blaffed up by Le Gommier, I declared a blanket amnesty for all the sea urchins that had ever attempted to puncture my feet in those small Mediterranean resorts with high infection rates and unshaven doctors.

"You're right, of course. You're right," I said to Alice.

"Can't you just sit down and relax?" she said. "Read a book or something."

"Of course you're right," I said. "I'll do that." I reached into the beach bag and withdrew a copy of Dr. André Nègre's *The French West Indies Through Their Cookery*.

I had some difficulty understanding how Alice could relax on a beach whose very snack bar offered eggs mimosa and *salade niçoise*. We were not, after all, on one of those Caribbean islands where the British spent a few centuries teaching the natives the art of large table settings and cool gray meat. We had served our time on those islands. Once, while we were living in a rented house on Tortola, Alice asked the storekeeper she had ordered a chicken from if he would cut it up for her, and returned to find that he had taken a frozen chicken and run it through a band saw. Alice, as I remember, said something on that occasion that sounded rather like "Blaff."

How could a person who had once been handed a chicken that looked like fifteen perfectly uniform pieces of thickly sliced bologna be so casual about spending her vacation in a place that has had entire books written about its cookery? I don't mean Alice was allowing herself to become malnourished. At La Grand' Voile, a distinguished Fort de France restaurant whose proprietor is from Lyons, she had casually downed an avocado with shrimp, a steak with morels, and an order of *cèpes*—a marvelous variety of French mushroom so large that an elf coming across one in the forest could climb up on it and address the other elves, up to his ankles in garlic and oil. She had missed no desserts. Between meals, though, she appeared to be in danger of backsliding into her old interest in the peripheral issues of travel—like touring the rain forest or lying on the beach. Fortunately, I was there to put her back on the track.

"Isn't it about time we cleaned up for lunch?" I asked. I had skipped rather quickly over a section of Dr. Nègre's book that seemed to carry West Indian authenticity a bit further than I wanted to go—it referred to "a bat worthy of the plate"—and had arrived at a passage that reminded me how close we were to a restaurant reputed to have a first-rate version of *blaff de poissons*.

"It's ten o'clock in the morning," Alice said. "We just had breakfast."

"We may have already stayed out too long in sun this strong," I said.

"But you're as pale as you were when we left New York," Alice said.

"Then it must have gone right through," I said. "Because I definitely have heartburn."

"Food isn't everything," Alice said the next morning. She had passed up the French toast soaked in rum she normally had for breakfast at the hotel, making do with a croissant or two, and she seemed to be feeling exceedingly virtuous, like a London air raid warden during the Second World War who had refrained from taking his full meat ration as a matter of principle.

"You're absolutely right, Alice," I said. "The French have never been able to make scrambled eggs worth a damn."

"You agreed that we would see some part of this island

16

that was not the inside of a restaurant," she said. "The rain forest. The volcano."

"Well, I thought the view of the Fort de France harbor from La Grand' Voile was quite picturesque," I said. "I suspect it seemed even more picturesque because of the way they took the avocado out of the shell, mixed it with some mysterious goodies in one of their ancient blenders, and put it back in. But I think it would have been picturesque anyway."

"Views from restaurants don't count."

I reminded her that just two days before we had stood in a quaint fishing village while the villagers hauled in their communal net—stood there for almost an hour before driving off to have some very satisfying *soupe de poissons* at the hotel in Diament les Bains. I've never minded watching fish being hauled in as long as such activity was preparatory to eating some. Was Alice implying that I had no interest in flora, fauna and fancy buildings? Who was it who took her to Chartres, while in the neighborhood searching out a stew of local renown?

On the other hand, I wanted Alice to have a lovely vacation. It is true that I hate scenery, but hadn't I been the one who said that marriage is sharing more than just your fettucine? "You're absolutely right, Alice," I finally said. "We should definitely take a drive around the island. We could end up in Morne-des-Esses for lunch; a lady there named Mrs. Palladino is supposed to serve spectacular crawfish." Crawfish, one of the fauna that had drawn us to Martinique, had turned out to be hard to find. I thought that the sea urchins I was gobbling down might soothe the longing for crawfish I had been nursing since my last trip to southwestern Louisiana—at one restaurant outside of Fort de

France, I had even devoured a sea urchin soufflé—but the true cure for a crawfish longing is crawfish.

Alice consulted the map. "That would actually be out of the way," she said.

"If there's one thing I believe, Alice," I said, "it's that no place that has spectacular crawfish is out of the way."

"The volcano in Martinique is really quite famous," Alice said, as we drove along the next morning. "It once erupted and killed thirty thousand people."

"All the more reason not to approach it," I said, pulling into the small mountain village of Morne-des-Esses. Both the volcano and the rain forest were a long way from Morne-des-Esses, but I had convinced Alice that we would still have time to see them if lunch turned out to be a quick snack.

Mrs. Palladino's restaurant, Le Colibri, amounted to a half-dozen tables on an open porch in the back of her house. The house appeared modest from the outside, but the porch looked out over some huge banana trees, and a mountain or two, and, a few miles away, the sea—a view that seemed picturesque to me even before Mrs. Palladino brought us some delicious *calalou des crabes*.

"I suppose we could just get some crawfish and dash off, Alice," I said. "But this is really like someone's house, and I hate to eat and run."

"I just hope you'll be able to walk," Alice said, watching me go after the second course—a torte made with minced conch. I knew she meant nothing by the remark. She wanted to protect me from overeating in the same way I wanted to protect her from a volcano that had once erupted and killed thirty thousand people.

18

Eventually, Mrs. Palladino returned with what she called *buisson d'écrevisses*—a bush of crawfish, formed by arranging half a dozen huge crawfish in a goblet, and accompanied by a creole sauce for dunking. As we polished off the crawfish, I discussed with Alice the problem created by a friend having phoned ahead to make certain that Mrs. Palladino served us some of our friend's favorite dishes. "If we leave now," I explained, "we'll never know what she might have brought out next." What she did bring out next was a stuffed pigeon, resting on a nest woven out of shoestring potatoes and accompanied by a purée of *christophene* —*christophene* being something I can describe only as what vegetables would be like if they were pure white and tasted good.

We had been eating for a couple of hours when Mrs. Palladino arrived to clear away the pigeon and inform us that dessert was fresh coconut flan. Alice sighed.

"When we talk about a rain forest, what are we really talking about, Alice?" I said. "What we're talking about is a bunch of wet trees."

Alice nodded, and turned to Mrs. Palladino and said in very good French, "We'll take two."

3

Stalking the Barbecued Mutton

I once wronged the state of Kentucky, but compared with the Kentucky Fried Chicken people I am an innocent. All I did was to pass on the information that a friend of mine named Marshall J. Dodge III—a man renowned on the East Coast for having somehow forged a successful career as a semiretired amateur folklorist—claimed that he had encountered the supreme fried chicken in a town called Rabbit Hash, Kentucky, while touring the area with a calliope restorer of his acquaintance. Local connoisseurs quickly point out that Marshall must have been thinking of a chicken restaurant in Cynthiana, Kentucky—Rabbit Hash being a place so small that the goods and services it offers the traveler probably don't extend to high-test. People I know in the state seemed satisfied with my explanation that Marshall is the sort of person who would never say

Cynthiana when he could say Rabbit Hash. I pointed out, as an example, that the friend Marshall always refers to as a calliope restorer might be described by most people as a piano dealer—although I believe the friend thinks of himself mainly as an actor and a semiprofessional blower of smoke rings.

A few years after the unfortunate misidentification of Cynthiana as Rabbit Hash, I told Alice that I was thinking about making further amends by journeying to Cynthiana and sampling a platter or two of the chicken in question.

"That sort of penance seems to be one of your specialties," Alice said.

"Well, naturally, I'd like to get this thing straightened out once and for all," I said. "There's nothing like a clear conscience."

I phoned a serious eater I know in Covington, Kentucky, and he informed me, in the sort of voice a heavy investor in Mexican savings banks might have used to discuss the drop in the peso that winter, that the Cynthiana restaurant had closed its doors. I was not surprised. In recent years legendary fried-chicken places seem to have closed at about the rate that indoor shopping malls open—Mrs. Stroud's, in Kansas City, and Mrs. Kremer's, near Jefferson City, just to toss off the names of two darkened shrines in my own home state. I suppose there were serious fried-chicken eaters in Kansas City who considered emigration after Mrs. Stroud's closed, but fortunately a successor appeared—a place called R. C.'s, which serves deep-fried chicken livers, and fried chicken with a strong, peppery batter, and potatoes with a marvelous suggestion of bacon grease that has, like an old retainer, been with the family for years. Someone who composed menus for those "Continental" restaurants that spin around on the top of bank buildings in places like Kansas City, endangering the superstructure with the weight of their sauces, would probably refer to R. C.'s potatoes as *pommes de terre à la bas église*, or potatoes in the Low Church manner.

Because a superior fried-chicken restaurant is often the institutional extension of a single chicken-obsessed woman, I realize that, like a good secondhand bookstore or a bad South American dictatorship, it is not easily passed down intact. Still, in sullen moments I blame these lamentable closings on the vertical integration of the broiler industry—the method by which one mass-producing corporation controls broilers from hatching to marketplace, keeping strict control on their tastelessness the entire time. In fact, in sullen moments I blame almost everything on the vertical integration of the broiler industry—the way some people trace practically any sort of mischief or natural disaster back to the Central Intelligence Agency, and some people, presumably slightly more sophisticated, blame everything on the interstate highway program. If the civilization is really about to crumble, everybody is entitled to his own idea of which is the most significant crack. Which brings us to Kentucky Fried Chicken.

Once, when I had the honor of accompanying Fats Goldberg to the Smithsonian Institution for the opening of an exhibition that included the neon sign saying GOLDBERG'S PIZZERIA as one of the artifacts assembled to remind us of the roots of our culture, both Fats and I noticed how much of the neon display was devoted to signs advertising American franchise restaurants in foreign languages. It occurred to me that Kentucky Fried Chicken is what a schoolboy in Osaka or a housewife in Brussels thinks fried chicken tastes like. The world may be growing smaller, but schoolboys in Osaka have never even heard of Mrs. Stroud. Kentucky Fried Chicken has become an international symbol of fast food, even though a chicken fried with care and respect is particularly slow food—pan-frying being a process that requires enough time to make any prospective diner begin worrying about whether he has come close to filling himself up with pickled watermelon rind and assorted relishes. It is also a symbol, I realized, of Kentucky—as if French cuisine were associated in the minds of all foreigners with the sort of frozen French fries dished out to hot rodders in greasy drive-ins. Are the Swiss thought of as people who sit around all the time eating what high-school dining halls in the Midwest call Swiss steak? Why should Kentucky be maligned?

"It hardly seems fair," I said to Alice.

"I suppose your sense of justice requires that you stuff yourself with something," Alice said.

She understands these matters. The reputation of Kentucky could be reclaimed, I decided, only if the people who spread the word about food were tipped off to a Kentucky specialty that would blot out memories of what Colonel Sanders himself has called "nothing but a fried doughball wrapped around some chicken." I resolved to seek out the barbecued mutton of western Kentucky—a unique regional delicacy I heard about when a restaurant tout wrote me to say that the menu of her favorite restaurant in Owensboro said, "Mary Had a Little Lamb. Won't You Have Some Too?"

"I'm calling from Horse Cave," I told Alice on the telephone a couple of nights later.

There was a long silence. "I thought you said barbecued mutton was a specialty of *western* Kentucky," Alice finally said. "According to the map, Horse Cave is in south-central Kentucky. The specialty there wouldn't be country ham, would it?"

"As a matter of fact, it would," I admitted. "But that does not happen to be the reason I'm here."

I began to understand what one of my fellow Traveling People—a drummer in electronic software, as I remember —meant when he told me that a conscientious husband on the road gets nothing for calling home every night but suspicious questions and reports of plumbing emergencies. As a traveler who had always looked forward to nightly calls home—even after the Chez Helène Incident—I was astonished to hear suspicion in the voice of my own wife, a person I would trust with my last fried dumpling. I'll admit that I would rather say Horse Cave than Owensboro, and I'll admit that I'd rather say country ham than almost anything if the person I was saying it to happened to be a waitress. But I had stopped off at Horse Cave for the perfectly legitimate purpose of seeking the advice of Tom Chaney, a reformed English professor who runs a corn-and-tobacco farm there with his Aunt Daisie Carter. Tom happens to be a practicing specialist in the eating of Kentucky foods.

It was perfectly natural that Tom and I and his Aunt Daisie, a cheerful lady who spent fifty-one years in the Hart County school system and seems none the worse for wear, held our first meeting while eating country ham. There is nothing suspicious about that. We had driven to a nearby town called Sulphur Well around noon, and pulled up at a small brick building identified on a Coke sign as Porter's— a place that had apparently inherited the local country-ham trade from the Beula Villa, an old hotel that used to serve as headquarters for people who drank the sulfuric water of the area to clear up whatever had been bothering them. I sampled the magic spring, and, just before we went into lunch, revealed to Chaney my suspicion that the reputation of Porter's might rest on the fact that anything would taste good after that water. But the ham turned out to be a triumph—sliced thin, and fried, and served with a bowl of redeye gravy. In fact, while we were eating at Porter's it occurred to me that country ham rather than barbecued mutton might be the local specialty that could put soggy fried chicken out of the public mind—until Mrs. Carter informed me that the most authentic country hams are illegal.

The actual ham we were wolfing down, she assured me, was quite within the law, but the sort of country ham that local people traditionally bought from a farmer—a farmer who might kill three or four hogs a year, cure the hams to sell, and use the rest of the meat for his own table—could no longer be sold legally because such farmers were obviously not set up to meet modern government meat-inspection standards.

"You mean the country ham you cook at home has to be bought from a supermarket?" I asked.

"Well, it's sort of like bootleg whiskey," Mrs. Carter told me, making it clear from her tone that she had not been the kind of schoolteacher who spent her spare time roaming the neighborhood kicking over stills and lecturing on the evils of Demon Rum.

I suddenly had a vision of Tom and his Aunt Daisie racing from their long-time supplier with three or four bootleg hams in the back seat, the Agriculture Department's version of revenuers in hot pursuit—Tom and Aunt Daisie tearing around curves, losing the law at last on the back roads they knew so well, and arriving home with the contraband they would cook secretly at night, hoping that the succulent aroma would not draw the authorities to their door. Knowing that people in some parts of Kentucky are still sensitive about their reputation for free-lance distilling, I could hardly draw attention to a product whose most authentic version was illegal. We each had two or three more pieces of ham while we talked it over. Then Tom asked me how the sulfur water had affected my health.

"I feel like a million," I said. "A little full, but like a million."

Tom was reminded of a legendary eater in Horse Cave named Miss Fannie Hiser, a large woman who used to live with his Aunt Minnie. After everybody had finished one of the huge Sunday dinners Miss Fannie prepared, Tom recalled, she used to lean back in her chair, fold her hands contentedly under her ample midsection, and say "Thank God for capacity."

"Are you sure this place we're going for dinner serves decent fried chicken?" I asked Tom late that afternoon. Tom had gathered some barbecued-mutton information by phone that day from an old college friend who grew up in Sturgis, Kentucky, right in the heart of the barbecued-mutton belt. We had arranged to go over the information while eating a fried-chicken supper with Tom's father, Boots Chaney, a more or less retired insurance man who remains fully active as a chicken eater. What had aroused my suspicion was Tom's choice of the concession restaurant in Mammoth Cave National Park—the sort of restaurant I have been suspicious of since Alice and a friend of ours waited forty-five minutes in a Bryce Canyon version for some broiled brook trout, only to discover when it finally arrived it had been broiling the entire time.

I was reassured when I noticed that the menu specified native chicken and a thirty-minute wait. "It's heartening to see that a restaurant in a national park is going to take the time to pan-fry some chicken," I told Tom. "It's the sort of thing that could help restore Americans' faith in their government." A necessary assumption in serving the slow-food variety of fried chicken is that the people waiting for it in the dining room are waiting with people they don't mind waiting with. Waiting for pan-fried chicken with the Chaneys is a treat. At the time of my visit they were sharing an office in Horse Cave—a two-room affair they sometimes referred to as Bogus Enterprises Inc.—and they have always shared a fondness for anecdotes about the area. Either of them could easily fill a half-hour pan-frying wait just with stories of the methods owners of the area's limestone caves once used to snatch tourists from each other, or just with stories about the adventures undergone by sane men trying to survive in a dry county. No wonder the people who emerge from fast-food emporiums look so sour: they probably haven't heard a good story in years.

The Chaneys are such splendid hosts that even though my comment on the fried chicken was an endorsement of some restraint ("The chicken is certainly no disgrace"), they offered to let me have one of their limited supply of country hams. I was loath to take it, knowing what I did about mad chases down tricky country roads, but I agreed to accompany Tom and Boots to Bogus Enterprises Inc. so that we could at least take a look at it. When we got to the office, Boots slid a pasteboard box from underneath one of the desks, and pulled a country ham out of it. The ham had been wrapped in newspapers, bits of which were still sticking to it. A country ham is not, at first glance, beautiful. Even without bits of newspaper, it is often covered by what appears to be mold and dirt. A cousin of mine who is from Kentucky had a friend who worked his way through the state college at Bowling Green uglying up ordinary hams to make them look like properly cured country hams—much the same way some ambitious young fellows in England work their way through school distressing wood to make eighteenth-century tables. (My cousin's friend, having successfully completed his degree, is now apparently working contentedly as a grave digger—a reminder that if Frank Merriwell or Dink Stover had lived in an age of downward mobility they might have followed up their college triumphs by becoming operators of a bead-and-leather shop.)

"I hate to take one of the few you have," I said, looking at the ham.

"You owe it to yourself," Tom said. "I'll even include the family country ham recipe." He immediately sat down and typed out the recipe, using some fancy stationery he had bought for his father which said B. T. Chaney on top and had across the bottom the legend "Widows Tended—Lies Told—Whiskey Hauled."

Boots Chaney assured me that the bits of newspaper sticking to the ham were the county paper of Hart County—adding to rather than detracting from the ham's authenticity.

"It's not that," I said. "I just know the trouble you go through to get one of these." Then I thought of something. "I'd be grateful to take it," I said.

I hauled the ham back to my motel and phoned Alice in New York. "I've got a gift for you, Alice," I said.

"Oh, how nice," she said. "Is it a surprise?"

"It's a surprise," I said. I had advised the software sales-man that it's the little touches like surprise, no-special-occasion gifts that keep the romance in a marriage.

I approached Owensboro warily. Barbecue is a touchy subject all over the country. Some of the regional quibbling on the subject can become ferocious, barbecue specialists being united only in the belief that the finest barbecue place in the country is Arthur Bryant's of Kansas City. The only serious question ever raised about Bryant's food turned out, to everyone's relief, to be nothing but a misunderstanding. It came in the summer of 1974. Alice, I remember, had gone back to New York from Nova Scotia for a couple of days that summer, and she returned bearing a copy of the *New York Times Sunday Magazine*. She said the magazine contained some harsh words about Arthur Bryant's. Alice has always been fond of Bryant's, but, perhaps because she was born and raised in the suburbs of New York, I have never completely erased the suspicion in my mind that she might be playing along a bit when it comes to barbecue eating—the way someone who married a maniac trout fish-erman might, all things considered, evidence more interest in the intricacies of fly-tying than she really felt. I have, after all, been with her at Bryant's when she stopped eating twenty or thirty minutes before I did, although in fairness I should say that the other people at the table stopped with her. She has been rather resistant to stories about the live-stock aspect of Kansas City culture—refusing to believe, for instance, that the cow on top of the American Hereford

Association building contains a heart and liver that light up at night. Sometimes, in those low hours we all have if we wake up just before dawn, I wonder if barbecue can really be appreciated by someone who can extract the heart of an artichoke as deftly as Alice can. Mixed marriages are not without their strains.

On this occasion, though, Alice seemed second to none in her loyalty to Arthur Bryant's. She turned to a piece by John and Karen Hess on American restaurants, and read out loud from their report on a visit to Arthur Bryant's: " 'To our taste the ham was very good—' "

"Well, I agree that's a rather bland response," I interrupted. "But Easterners are known for understatement."

" '—the beef poor and greasy, and the famous spareribs edible but dry and disappointing.' "

I was, I admit, taken aback. We knew the Hesses to be serious people of the sort I believe French intellectuals refer to as *premiers fressers*—a distinguished couple who . . . Suddenly, I understood what had happened. I immediately sat down and wrote a letter to the *Times Magazine* which read, in part, "At Bryant's, it has always been the custom of the counterman to pick up the ribs in his right hand and toss them on the plate he pulls toward him with his left hand—a motion he has perfected in a career of some twenty-eight years. When the counter was approached by Mr. and Mrs. Hess—a distinguished-looking couple if ever there was one—the counterman obviously was sufficiently awed to serve the ribs with a pair of tongs that are used for special occasions and were last employed, I believe, during a visit to Kansas City in 1937 by Emperor Haile Selassie of Ethiopia. Alas, what everyone in Kansas City knows and someone should certainly have thought to tell Mr. and Mrs.

Hess is that the taste of the ribs is partly in the counterman's hand."

Even with the matter of supremacy settled to everyone's satisfaction, I knew I could encounter some defensiveness in Owensboro. Americans argue not just about whose barbecue is second-best but even about what barbecue is. In the Southwest, for instance, people ordinarily barbecue ribs, but in North Carolina the word is used as a noun referring only ·to chopped pork that has been flavored, in a manner of speaking, with a vinegar-based sauce. It is normal for regional loyalists to be both chauvinistic and arcane when talking about the local version. Griffin Smith, who had a distinguished career as Barbecue Editor of *The Texas Monthly*, has, after research that some considered excessive, managed to divide Texas barbecue into sauce and non-sauce categories—the non-sauce people looking down on the sauce types as people who have every reason to disguise the flavor of their meat. I once talked to some North Carolina expatriates in New York about barbecue, after returning from a short visit to their home state, and found myself subjected to stern geographical probings:

"Were you east of Rocky Mount?"

"Is Goldsboro east of Rocky Mount?"

"West. There's no decent barbecue west of Rocky Mount."

"I don't know where Rocky Mount is, but it must be east of all the towns I ate barbecue in."

"I expect so."

Although I assumed that people in Owensboro would be proud of their local version—not just a different sort of pork or a different way of slicing beef but an entirely different animal—it also occurred to me that Owensboro might not want to be proclaimed "Barbecued-Mutton Capital of the World." It's a fairly sophisticated town, after all, with four distilleries, and a General Electric plant that was turning out more than half a million tubes a day before it was struck low by the Japanese transistor, and two colleges, and a river port on the Ohio, and a thirteen-story motel just as perfectly round as a good silo. Baffling as it may seem, there are residents of Cincinnati who are not pleased when I refer to their city as the Center of Greek Chili in Ohio.

In cities the size of Cincinnati and Kansas City, food like barbecue and chili remains an embarrassment to people who want to think of themselves as living in a big-league city that is sophisticated enough to have an array of Continental restaurants—Continental restaurants that are modeled, an unwary traveler can discover, on the continent of Antarctica, where everything starts out frozen. A friend of mine who once wandered into Kansas City on the lecture circuit asked his hosts to take him to Arthur Bryant's—expressing at the same time his thankfulness for at last having the opportunity to visit what has been identified as the single greatest restaurant in the world. His hosts refused. They were apparently among those people in Kansas City afflicted with a disease of the American provinces I have managed to isolate and identify as rubaphobia—not the fear of rubes but the fear of being thought of as a rube. Rubaphobiacs would not think of taking someone as important as an itinerant lecturer to a barbecue joint whose main dining room has no decorations beyond an eye chart. (I have always assumed that the eye chart is there to give customers some way of determining when they have had enough of Mr. Bryant's barbecue sauce. It is, at any rate, what a New York designer might call "elegant in its simplicity.") In a city that "boasts," as they always say, so many restaurants advertising Continental Cuisine, how can one take an out-of-town visitor to a restaurant that identifies itself as the House of Good Eats? They took him instead to the Arrowhead Club of the Harry S Truman Sports Complex (a football stadium standing next to a baseball stadium, as if the builder couldn't get it right the first time and tried again), where, he has since testified, he ate what the menu described as "a fish of the Pacific waters."

Still, I had some reason to believe that Owensboro would not mind being the Barbecued-Mutton Capital of the World. Rubaphobia is much more prevalent in towns of a half million than in towns of fifty thousand. But it did occur to me that Owensboro might already have a slogan that it would be reluctant to part with.

"No, I think slogans for cities are trite," the executive vice president of the Chamber of Commerce told me. "We don't have one anymore."

"What did the slogan used to be?"

"Opportunity Center of the U. S. A."

"I see what you mean. But you do think that Owensboro is—in fact, if not in slogan—the barbecued-mutton capital of the world?"

"Undoubtedly," he said.

Two hours later Tom Chaney, who had been doing some further checking with specialists from Union County, informed me by telephone from Horse Cave that Waverly, Kentucky, forty-five miles west of Owensboro, might be the barbecued-mutton capital of the world. Not an hour after that, the proprietor of Posh & Pat's, a barbecue place in Henderson, on the way to Waverly, said of Owensboro,

"They've got the reputation, we've got the barbecue." Meanwhile, I had been told that the premier barbecue mutton was served by a man named Woolfolk in Cairo, Kentucky, just south of Henderson, but only in the summer. I knew I had come to the right territory.

"How come this is the only area where mutton is barbecued?" I asked an Owensboro merchant who had been kind enough to give me change for a nickel parking meter.

"I expect because there are so many Catholics here," he said.

I didn't want to appear ignorant. "Yeah," I said. "I suppose that'd do it."

As I was searching my mind for some connection between the Roman rite and mutton consumption, the merchant told me that the large Catholic churches in town have always staged huge picnics that feature barbecue and burgoo—burgoo, another staple of Owensboro barbecue restaurants, being a soupy stew that I had always associated with southern Illinois. In the early days the church picnics apparently served barbecued goat. In fact, Owensboro might have arrived at barbecued mutton by a process of elimination, since people in the area seem willing to barbecue just about any extant mammal. In western Kentucky, barbecue restaurants normally do "custom cooking" for patrons who have the meat but not the pit, and among the animals that Posh & Pat's offers to barbecue is raccoon. The Shady Nest, one of the most distinguished barbecue joints in Owensboro ("We have people in here from all over," the waitress told me. "We had a Puerto Rican in here once"), has a sign that says, "If It Will Fit on the Pit, We Will Barbecue It." It is probably fortunate that people in west-

ern Kentucky settled on barbecued mutton as the local delicacy before they had a go at porcupine or bollweevil.

I started eating barbecued mutton. I tried the Moonlite,
which barbecues eight hundred pounds of mutton a day,
and I tried lunch counters that probably don't account for
the demise of more than a sheep or two a week. I ate sliced
mutton. I ate chopped mutton. I ate mutton ribs. My find-
ings confirmed the natural law that the shape of an object
has limited effect on its taste. I liked barbecued mutton, but,
then, I might have liked barbecued porcupine, Alice's theory being that the taste I truly crave is the taste of hickory-
wood smoke.

After only six or eight meals of barbecued mutton, I had
prepared the report I would give the first internationally
influential eater I ran across. I tried it out on Alice when I
called home that night. "They serve barbecued mutton just
about every way," I said. "Sliced, chopped, ribs, hidden in
burgoo."

"Is it good?" she asked.

"It's not bad at all."

"Just 'not bad at all'?" she said. "You had six or eight
meals of it today, and it's just 'not bad at all'?"

"I believe I prefer it to Greek chili," I said. "Also, as far
as I know, it is, unlike country ham, not illegal in its most
authentic form."

Barbecued mutton is, as the saying goes, not Kansas
City, but there are reasons not to apply such standards. In
Posh & Pat's, after all, the restaurant gossip going on when I
walked in was not about someone's secret sauce formula
but about the Burger Farm franchise just down the interstate being replaced by a Wiener King. A local restaurant

man who happened to be at Posh & Pat's counter downing a sliced-mutton sandwich said he was thinking of opening a new steak restaurant with an "old depot" décor. "It's all Western or Barn here now," he told me. With the franchisers and the décor-mongers closing in, any authentic local specialty obviously needed celebrating. Did I want a nice river city like Owensboro—a city that, according to my calculations, has a barbecued-mutton restaurant for every 5,188 residents—to be known as the Ex-Tube Capital of the World? Was it fair to serious eaters in Kentucky— the Chaneys, for instance—that foreigners should believe their state to be nothing but a jungle of fast-food franchises like Burger Farm and Wiener King? "Kentucky is the Barbecued-Mutton Capital of the World," I would tell the first eater of influence I could find. "Spread the word."

Not a month later, Tom Eblen, a renowned Kansas City rib-eater I happened to be talking to on the telephone, said, "What's this you're spreading about barbecued mutton being unique to western Kentucky?"

"That's right," I said, delighted that the word had reached an authority of Eblen's stature so quickly. "Barbecued-Mutton Capital of the World."

"You know who serves barbecued mutton?" Eblen said. "Arthur Bryant's. They've had it on the menu for years."

I was momentarily stunned. "How would I be expected to know that?" I finally said. "I've never had occasion to look at the menu at Bryant's. I've been ordering the same thing since I was fourteen."

Since my talk with Eblen I have consciously avoided testing Bryant's barbecued mutton. If it is up to Mr. Bryant's usual standards, Kansas City would also be the Barbecued-Mutton Capital of the World, and that hardly seems fair.

4
To Market,
To Market

Jeffrey Jowell, a friend of ours who teaches law at the University of London, likes to go to the Friday morning market at Barnstaple to chat about poultry and eggs. "You say a bit of peat on the floor of the coop?" he will ask a farmer's wife, staring at her with the sort of intent look that law professors must dream of finding on the faces of their students during a lecture. "How very interesting!" I have never missed an opportunity to go to the Barnstaple market with Jeffrey, although it also happens to be true that I have never missed an opportunity to go to any market with anyone at any time. I love weekly markets, even when they do not offer the added attraction of a law professor discussing chicken feed with a vendor of brown eggs. Wandering through the Friday morning market at Barnstaple—poking at fresh tomatoes or bargaining for what is purported to be an antique clipboard or munching on some Farmhouse Cheddar to keep up my strength between stalls—I occasionally pause to wonder why all of the other tourists are at Buckingham Palace or the Tower of London. Alice is also enthusiastic about the Barnstaple market, although the suspicion lingers that when she seems to be completely absorbed in selecting peaches she is actually glancing over now and then to make certain that I make no overt attempt to corner the North Devon scone market.

A Friday morning at Barnstaple is definitely enhanced by the opportunity to hear Jeffrey say, "Yes, laying very well at the moment, thanks," to an egg vendor, inspecting the color of her shells rather closely as he speaks. When the university is not in session, Jeffrey and his family live near Exford, a Somerset village about an hour's drive from Barnstaple. During their first summer there, we were informed by letter that Jeffrey, whose interest in husbandry had previously escaped our notice, had finished second in the other-than-white egg division of the Exford and District Flower and Produce Show. Jeffrey did not take the victory lightly, even though, we later learned, the other-than-white egg division of the Exford and District Flower and Produce Show had only three entries. According to the reports we got from England, Jeffrey talked a lot about chickens and he talked a lot to chickens. "Good night, ladies," he would say each evening when he shut his hens into their coop, safe from marauding foxes. "Sleep well, my lovelies." Jeffrey's wife, Francie, even reported that on visits to neighbors in Somerset Jeffrey had taken to cracking eggs he found in the pantry and sneering at their yolks. I wasn't certain whether Francie was joking until we arrived in England for a visit, about a year after Jeffrey had acquired his flock, and noticed on the desk in his study, in the sort of frame some people might use for a picture of their wife and children, a five-by-seven-inch color portrait of Rudolph, his rooster.

We attended the second Exford and District Flower and Produce Show that Jeffrey entered, and I was with him when he learned, to his great dismay, that he had fallen to third place in the other-than-white egg division.

"Look on the bright side," I said, trying to cheer him up. "There were four entries this year, so in a way you did just as well as you did last time—second from last."

Francie offered some token condolences, but she does not like to encourage what she occasionally calls Jeffrey's "obsession." I can't blame her. It was presumably her picture, after all, that was on Jeffrey's desk before Rudolph came along. Also, it must be embarrassing for Francie to be sitting quietly at a neighbor's dinner table when suddenly her husband snatches an egg from the pantry, cracks it into the dish the hostess was planning to use for the custard, and begins a lecture on causes of yolk paleness. Francie has been known to make light of Jeffrey's career in poultry management. She was among those on a panel of Jeffrey's family and friends—a panel on which Alice and I also had the privilege of serving—that, after some informal calculations, priced out the cost of Jeffrey's home-grown, economical eggs at "one pound fifty per egg, plus a hundred points of cholesterol." She has neither confirmed nor denied rumors that she may have been privy to a conspiracy—a conspiracy that Alice and I had the privilege of devising and successfully carrying out—by which some London supermarket eggs were secretly substituted for the freshly gathered eggs that Jeffrey was about to serve his guests as examples of what fresh farm eggs should taste like. (Jeffrey later denied that he had been completely fooled; he has not denied that the next time we arrived in Exford from London all of the eggs in his pantry had been marked with his tiny initial.) At some point, Francie began referring to Jeffrey as Chicken George.

These days, of course, there is nothing particularly unusual about a law professor being deeply involved in poultry raising. It wouldn't surprise me, in fact, to find that in some Midwestern university professors of agricultural science, who were once thought of by the liberal arts faculty as ranking just above phys. ed. majors, are now sought as dinner guests by the chairman of the Philosophy Department, who hopes they might share some of their erudition in the area of soil preparation or slug eradication. Academics have their own way of approaching agriculture: Jeffrey, according to my last count, owns at least fourteen books and several pamphlets on poultry keeping. He has read *Starting Poultry Keeping* and he has read *The Small Commercial Poultry Flock* (Technical Bulletin #198 issued by the Ministry of Agriculture, Fisheries and Food). He sometimes says that the sight of his chickens taking their first tentative steps into the sunlight—they had been kept by their previous owner in cages, and Jeffrey decided to allow them to roam the farm as what the English call "free-range hens"—reminded him of the prisoners' chorus in *Fidelio*, an image I have never heard used by the farmers' wives who sell eggs at the Barnstaple market.

Although professors may reach for an operatic image to describe a barnyard phenomenon, it must be even more common for them to discover that what they had assumed was a metaphor is simply a fact of rural life. My own experience with the agricultural sciences in Nova Scotia is limited to a little experiment I'm carrying out on levels of production in totally neglected apple trees, but I am occasionally astonished anew to find that a neighbor who mentions the need to prime the pump is talking not about tinkering with the free-market economy but about priming the pump. People in Nova Scotia do make hay, and if at all possible, they make it while the sun shines so that it will be dry when they store it in the barn. One day in Nova Scotia Alice came home with the information that one widely used method of improving apple production was to gather up all the windfalls every autumn—gather up not unearned and sudden profit but apples that had been caused by the wind to fall. (I decided against it, on the theory that it was the sort of behavior that could invalidate the results of my experiment.)

"Rudolph, you might say, rules the roost," Jeffrey told me the first time he showed me his flock settling in for the night. Jeffrey also mentions now and then that his flock actually does have a pecking order—one that he can recite, as it happens, since he has given each chicken the name of one of his cousins. Jeffrey's barnyard observations on the matter of pecking order are, of course, buttressed by a certain amount of scholarly research. It is from reading a book —*The Chicken Book*, by Page Smith and Charles Daniel— that he knows that the phenomenon of pecking order was discovered earlier in this century by a Norwegian psychologist named T. Schjelderup-Ebbe. I sent him the book. Jeffrey once mentioned the possibility of commissioning some local potter to fashion eggcups bearing the Clarence Day quotation that it uses as an epigraph—"Oh, who that ever lived and loved can look upon an egg unmoved?"

"You will most certainly not," Francie said at the time. "This obsession has gone far enough."

Francie, I think, might make light of Jeffrey's poultry

library except that she has, in addition to a doctorate in the history of art from Harvard, at least twenty-one books on gardening. She has *V. Sackville-West's Garden Book* and she has *Potatoes* (Technical Bulletin #94 issued by the Ministry of Agriculture, Fisheries and Food). She has entered the Exford and District Flower and Produce Show in as many as eleven categories at once, including such exotic competitions as Three Turnips and Four Sticks of Rhubarb. She does not bid her vegetables good night every evening, as far as I know, but I have heard her refer to store-bought provisions as "foreign vegetables" in the same tone of voice some British politicians use these days when referring to immigrants from the Indian subcontinent. In one Exford show, she won first prizes in both Heaviest Marrow and Two Matching Vegetable Marrows—a marrow being what the English call a large squash. Jeffrey occasionally refers to her as the Marrow Queen of Exford.

I have always been partial to market people. In England the difference between market people and shopkeepers is particularly pronounced. The grocers in Exford or Dunster or Taunton or Barnstaple strike me as the sort of correct English shopkeepers who find their greatest fulfillment in telling the customer who wants bread "The bread's finished" and informing the customer who asks for bacon "We don't do bacon, thank you very much." The people behind the tables that are lined up every Friday morning at Barnstaple may be rather quiet by the standards of, say, the Italian fruit-and-vegetable peddlers who appear at the Haymarket in the North End of Boston every Friday and Saturday, but, compared to most English shopkeepers, they take a positively overt pleasure in selling their wares. In

Barnstaple on Friday mornings, Jeffrey is not called Mr.
Jowell by the vendors but "my dear" or "my love." Informal, even intimate address is the norm at markets every-
where; I suspect that the only female customers not ad-
dressed as "honey" by vendors in the Haymarket are those
wearing nuns' habits. Once, when Alice and I were moving
slowly with a Saturday jam of people in the Haymarket, a
man who looked to be in his late seventies stepped forward,
kissed Alice warmly on both cheeks, and said in a heavy
Italian accent, "I would like to bring you home to meet my
mother."

As much as I like the atmosphere at markets, I go mainly
for the food. In the United States these days, some people
shop at a market on the theory that it represents their only
hope of coming across fruit and vegetables that have not
been bred by the agribusiness Frankensteins to have a shelf
life approximately that of a mop handle. They hope, for
instance, to find a tomato that does not have a bright-red
skin so hard that anyone who wanted to indulge in the old-
fashioned American pleasure of slinging it at a windy political stump speaker would risk being arrested for assault
with intent to kill. By the time American consumers began
to take serious notice of such matters, of course, ninety percent of the broilers available in grocery stores were already
being produced by agribusiness corporations that had discovered the cost-effectiveness of vertical integration. The
English who are always chastising themselves these days for
economic stagnation and failure to adopt modern management practices fail to realize that what they have avoided is
the vertical integration of the broiler industry.

A lot of vegetables sold at the Barnstaple market taste
more like vegetables than shelf displays simply because they

are the product of a kitchen garden rather than an assembly line. Although there are stalls at the market that sell great quantities of fruit and vegetables acquired from wholesalers, it is not unusual to come across a farmer's wife standing behind a table that holds, say, three dozen eggs, one chicken, three bunches of carrots, some beetroot, five turnips, six baby cabbages, a bunch of rhubarb, one marrow, a jar of apple chutney, and a jar of quince jelly. Barnstaple does not have the sort of customers who demand to know whether a cucumber or a radish has been grown under conditions the Natural Food Fanatics would consider "organic," but some of the eggs at the market carry prominent signs labeling them "free range." In England, consciousness of free-range eggs extends from vendors at provincial markets to gourmet stores in Knightsbridge that label eggs "free range" and leave enough grit and hay sticking to them to support the claim. A preference for free-range eggs is based partly on the theory that a chicken that spends its life roaming around a barnyard instead of being crammed into the wire cages used for what are called battery or factory or deep-litter hens is a healthier fowl that is likely to produce a better egg. But in England, where concern for dumb animals is so acute that there may well be people willing to picket beekeepers for keeping their bees in crowded conditions, part of the steam of the Free Range egg movement comes from groups with names like Chicken Lib—groups that object to hens leading a "thoroughly miserable existence." According to the brochure of an organization called Compassion in World Farming, factory farm animals "degrade the sensibilities of all who work with them," while free-range animals "through their active self-expression . . . make a valuable contribution to the countryside scene."

"Oh, you mustn't coop them up," an egg vendor at Barnstaple once told us. "With free-range hens the yolks are that much richer altogether."

"My first hens had been deep-litter hens, and I set them free," Jeffrey told her. She nodded and smiled. Jeffrey beamed. The emancipator.

The last time we were in Somerset, Jeffrey and Alice and I went to Barnstaple early one Friday morning for the market, leaving Francie home to tend her marrows. Francie asked us to be a restraining influence on Jeffrey, who had apparently gone off to a supermarket to do some marketing not long before and, seized by the zeal that foodstuffs bring out in him, had managed to spend seventy pounds on groceries—mumbling, in response to Francie's chastisement, something about the difficulty of coping with an inflationary economy. Jeffrey said he was interested in arranging to buy two or three chicks at the market if he could find a farmer's wife whose egg display met his standards. I didn't even have that excuse. I was interested in acquiring whatever I could to eat. I have never been to an open market that did not have something remarkable to eat. I believe it is fair to say that the West Country of England is not internationally renowned for its food, but I have always found marvelous food at the Barnstaple market—hardcakes baked by members of the Women's Institute, for instance, or a marrow we once came across that is known locally as spaghetti squash, or runner-bean chutney, or some liver dumplings called faggots, or a regional delicacy called, indelicately, hog's pudding.

Alice's response to her first look at hog's pudding had not been encouraging. "This happens to be a regional delicacy,

Alice," I said. "If we don't at least try it, Jeffrey might be hurt. You know how sensitive he is."

Alice fried the hog's pudding to a crisp crust, the same way she treats country scrapple we bring back from Pennsylvania. Even she acknowledged that the results were magnificent. I like a person who can admit she was wrong, I told Alice, particularly if that person can also cook scrapple.

As Jeffrey searched for a trustworthy purveyor of chicks that Friday morning, I wandered from booth to booth with a large market basket under my arm. Jeffrey was putting a few things in a market basket himself, and Alice volunteered to make a detailed inspection of the fish and meat available in a line of shops across from the market known as Butcher's Row. We had thought we were just picking up a few odds and ends, but when we returned to Exford and unpacked our market baskets in the Jowells' kitchen—carefully observed by Francie, who was presumably guarding against infiltration by foreign vegetables—we found that we had three jars of honey, one jar of raspberry jam, two cabbages, a jar of pickled onions, some Cheshire and Caerphilly and Cheddar cheese, a half-dozen honey lollipops, a carton of raspberries, a carton of blackberries, a bunch of bananas, a jar of tomato relish, an astounding number of shortbread cookies, a package of clotted cream, some bread pudding, a few tomatoes, a pound of hog's pudding, a pound of sunflower nuts, some extra-fruit strawberry jam, a lemon cheesecake, a half-dozen rock cakes, some fresh salmon, some fresh haddock, a cooked crab, six scones, a jar of runner-bean chutney, a jar of loganberry jam, one melon, a second jar of raspberry jam, three toy horses, one toy car, a jar of olive oil, a bunch of grapes, some sunflower oil, some wine vinegar, a pineapple cheesecake, even more rock cakes, three kippers, two smoked mackerels, a knitted hat, two hundred-weights of chicken feed, a few lemons, and half a faggot—another faggot and a half having been consumed in the heat of shopping.

Francie looked at Jeffrey and then at me. "Alice was the one who bought the salmon," I said weakly.

"Well," Jeffrey said. "We needed everything."

"Yes, I suppose so," Francie said. "We couldn't have lasted another day without those sunflower nuts."

Alice and I went back to Barnstaple with Jeffrey the following Friday so that he could pick up his chicks and I could replenish my hog's pudding supply—perhaps picking up some more Cheddar and another jar or two of runner-bean chutney as long as I was in the neighborhood. At one of the stalls three chicks, in a pasteboard box, were waiting for Jeffrey. On the ride back to Exford, his only two concerns about them were that they might be cocks rather than pullets and that they might not be chickens of any kind. They were odd-looking little gray birds that were supposedly of the Maran variety of chicken but suggested to the untrained eye—the kind of eye Jeffrey happens to have —baby hawks, or perhaps vultures.

"Determining the sex of chicks has only been success-fully done on a regular basis by the Koreans," Jeffrey said, apparently having pulled that fact out of *Natural Poultry Management* or *The Complete Poultry Keeper and Farmer*.

"I don't suppose you're going to be able to find any Koreans in Exford," I said. "Maybe in Taunton."

"Well, they're lovely little chicks anyway," Jeffrey said. I gathered from his remarks that he had decided to assume that the predatory-looking creatures in the back of the car were in fact chickens.

He slowed in the traffic leaving Barnstaple, and pointed

toward a car in front of us that was towing a trailer containing a calf. "That's my next venture," he said.

"Does Francie know about this?" Alice asked.

"Lovely thing, that," Jeffrey continued. "Lovely. I once fell in love with a Jersey cow at the Dunster Show."

5

Fly Frills to Miami

My decision to take a rather elegant picnic along on my no-frills flight to Miami was solidly based on a theory of economics known as Alice's Law of Compensatory Cashflow, which holds that any money not spent on a luxury one considered even briefly is the equivalent of windfall income and should be spent accordingly. If you decide, for instance, that buying a five-hundred-dollar color television set would be, all things considered, an act of lunacy and the final step toward complete financial collapse, you have an extra five hundred dollars that you "saved" on the television set available to spend on something else.

I'll admit that for several years I had some difficulty grasping the fine points of Alice's Law of Compensatory Cashflow. Alice would say something like "We have that five hundred dollars we saved on the television set," and I would nod quietly, meanwhile patting various pockets in a desperate effort to find it. I was not surprised at my difficulty in catching on. My own grasp of economics and finance is so tenuous that the fantasy I have during those blank moments aboard airplanes—when the plastics salesman sitting next to me is probably having a fantasy about being pursued by a sex-starved gang of Hollywood starlets who won't take no for an answer—is that all of our family's financial transactions are handled by a first cousin I have invented, a mildly wonky but lovable financial wizard named Harvey. In my fantasies, Harvey comes over to the house now and then for dinner when we are having one of his favorites—shad roe, maybe, or blintzes donated by Alice's Aunt Sadie. He always brings Alice flowers, smiling his awkward, wonky smile when he hands them to her. Abigail loves the nonsense poems Cousin Harvey recites to her. He is patiently trying to teach Sarah to wiggle her left ear. Dinner conversation is mainly remembering old times in Kansas City—like the time my sister, Sukey, one of Harvey's favorites, tried to toss me down the laundry chute. At some point, though, Harvey may say something like, "By the way, bubbele"—he has always called me bubbele—"we prepaid your New York State quarterly to take advantage of the shelter you got when we took you out of ball bearings and put you into frozen pork bellies and took care of the American Express bill you forgot to pay."

"Fine, Harv," I always say, idly. "Would you mind passing the sour cream?"

I began to understand the advantages of Alice's Law of Compensatory Cashflow rather suddenly one day when I realized that saving thirty-three dollars over coach fare or seventy-one dollars over first class by doing without the affliction of an airline meal on no-frills service called for spending at least thirty-three dollars and perhaps seventy-one dollars on a decent picnic lunch to see me through the flight.

"Just because you saved thirty-three dollars doesn't mean you necessarily have to spend it on food," Alice said.

"Every theory needs a corollary," I told her.

Having absorbed Alice's Law at last, I climbed on board a flight to Miami carrying, among other necessities, a small jar of fresh caviar, some smoked salmon I had picked up at a "custom smokery" in Seattle the week before, *crudités* with pesto dipping sauce, tomato-curry soup, butterfish with shrimp *en gelée*, spiced clams, lime and dill shrimp, tomatoes stuffed with guacamole, marinated mussels, an assortment of pâté, stuffed cold breast of veal, a bottle of Puligny-Montrachet, a selection of chocolate cakes, some praline cheesecake, and a dessert made from Italian cheese-in-the-basket and fresh strawberries and Grand Marnier by Alice —that rare example of an economic theorist who can also cook.

I am not among those people who have difficulty eating on airplanes because of anxieties connected with flying. As someone who travels constantly in the course of business, I naturally have no fears or superstitions brought on by being in an airplane; years ago, I discovered that I could keep the plane I was flying on from crashing by refusing to adjust my watch to the new time zone until we were on the ground, and I have used that method ever since. My only anxiety while flying off somewhere in an airplane has to do with being able to find the airport for the flight back. In a lot of American cities, the location of the airport is the final municipal secret. A traveling salesman who starts out in his rental car toward the airport, dreading the time he will have to spend in a place so purposefully designed to make human beings miserable, can take some perverse comfort in the fact that he probably won't be able to find it anyway. Occasionally, sitting in an airplane that is taking me to one city or another, I began to have visions of what I will go through in a few days trying to get back—desperately steering my rental car in what I judge by the sun to be the right direction, switching lanes suddenly to ask guidance from a policeman who turns out to be a deaf-mute, taking dangerously sudden turns onto thruways that lead to interchanges with other thruways that eventually end abruptly at Vista Vue Estates, model home open. Will the Bob Blakely Field referred to in the sign with an arrow pointing to the right but too close to the intersection to make a turn possible be the type of field from which airplanes take off—the city airport, perhaps—or the type of field upon which nine-year-old boys try to strike each other out for the glory of their parents? Could it really be that a road-sign symbol that looks like an airplane is being used to guide travelers to the municipal water-treatment plant? In a just world, any city that did not clearly mark the way to its airport would automatically lose its major-league franchise.

Kansas City used to have an airport that was practically walking distance from downtown. Then a gang of rubaphobiacs—the sort of people who would sooner lose the fire department than the major-league franchise; the same people who hired a New York public relations firm to persuade everyone that Kansas City was a "cow town no longer"—decided that what a "glamour city" like Kansas City could not do without was a $250 million "international airport." The city council annexed some land that seemed to be more appropriate for a suburb of Omaha—the city council's policy on accumulation of noncontiguous land having been inherited intact from the British Colonial Office of 1843—and the old airport quickly became part of our shameful cow-town past. I was outraged. I loved the old airport. I liked the name, Kansas City Municipal, which sounded like the sort of tax-free bond Cousin Harvey talks about now and then. I liked the approach over downtown Kansas City. Mostly, I loved landing so close to town that a native son who had a twenty-minute stopover before returning to the East could be met by a relief column bearing real barbecued ribs, still warm from their exposure to an authentic hickory-wood fire.

Driven to extremes by thoughts of how many pounds of Arthur Bryant's barbecue I would be deprived of over the years, I pointed out, in public print, that Kansas City International did not happen to have any flights that took off from its runways and landed on foreign soil. It was a spiteful revelation, and I regretted it almost immediately. Who wants to be in the position of knocking his own hometown —particularly such a splendid hometown, a hometown virtually flawless except for the presence of a few people who want to turn it into a bad imitation of Houston? Who wants to reveal that his own hometown lacks the savvy to cover itself in such a situation by bribing some place like Matamoros to take a flight or two? The people who so dread the thought of living in a cow town, I realized, are actually as fond of Kansas City as I am, in their own warped way. I finally even realized what they hated about the old airport: the landing approach I loved exposed the stockyard cattle pens and the cow on the top of the American Hereford

Association—not to mention a line of grain elevators and a World War One monument that, by the purest chance, happens to look like a grain elevator—to any sneering sales representative from New Jersey who happened to have a window seat. I suppose the rubaphobiacs love Kansas City, but mostly they just hate cows.

What usually keeps me from eating on an airplane is not anxiety but the food I'm served. I cannot say I have never had a good meal off the ground. Once, just before we left New Orleans, Alice had the inspired idea of stopping at Buster Holmes' restaurant, on Burgundy Street, to pick up some garlic chicken for the flight. It occurred to me that while we were about it we might as well stop at the Acme for an oyster loaf—a half-dozen succulent oysters freshly fried and installed in buttered French bread.

"Aren't you always saying that oyster loaves won't travel more than twenty yards from the kitchen?" Alice said. "They would be awful on the plane."

"Who's talking about the plane?" I said. "Have you given any thought to what we're going to eat on the way to the airport?" Every theory needs a corollary.

Buster's chicken had been, as usual, a triumph, but a picnic as elaborate as the one I had prepared for my flight to Miami was a new departure in air-travel eating for me. I'll admit that I took some steps to conceal my treasures from my fellow passengers. I think I am as generous as the next person about sharing certain kinds of food: if trapped by an avalanche in a mountain shack, I'm sure I would split my last few pieces of, say, packaged white bread or institutional roast beef with my fellow trappees, figuring that a natural disaster was always a good opportunity to

take off a pound or two. I had, however, taken pains
not to include in my no-frills picnic any of the type of
food I would share. For that reason I planned to carry it in
a squat briefcase once given to me by a part-time peddler of
home-improvement business courses—a briefcase that has
always caused people on subway platforms to edge away
from me, as if I were about to whip out an *Encyclopedia
Americana* and tell them that they owed their children a
home filled with culture and learning, suitably bound. As it
turned out, though, my eyes were bigger than my briefcase.
By the time everything was packed, I found myself carrying
a sort of annex to the briefcase in the form of a large shopping bag from my purveyor of caviar (and, on simpler occasions, of chopped herring and smoked salmon), Russ &
Daughters—casually trying to keep my newspaper over the
part of the bag that carried Russ's irresistible motto
"Queens of Lake Sturgeon."

I need not have bothered. Even when I offered the man
sitting behind me some caviar—an uncharacteristic gesture
prompted by his loan of a nail clipper to pry open the
caviar jar—he declined. The woman in the aisle seat across
from mine gazed longingly at my marinated mushrooms,
but only shook her head nervously when I offered her one. I
finally realized that my fellow passengers—chewing away
at what people unfamiliar with Alice's Law would think of
as a sensible lunch of, say, a chicken sandwich and a Tab—
assumed they were in the presence of a maniac, a man who
might get a kick out of slipping giggle powder into some
spiced clams before he offered them to an innocent traveler.
While I was eating my caviar and smoked-salmon course,
the woman sitting at the window two seats away from me—
the seat between us being empty except for two cartons of

my food—glanced over now and then with a suspicious but not unfriendly look, the way someone might look at the fellow at the Fourth of July picnic who insists, after a few beers, that everyone form a pyramid on the table he has balanced on his stomach.

She turned out to be a good-humored lady named Mrs. Eve Infeld, who, after attending to some family business in New York, was returning to Miami Beach, where her husband was semiretired in the garment game. She did not speak to me until we became co-conspirators—the stewardess's reminder about a regulation against drinking out of one's own bottle on an airliner having forced me, after some token resistance ("Are you sure that rule is meant to apply to Puligny-Montrachet?"), to secrete the bottle between my briefcase and Mrs. Infeld's shopping bag. I had to fill my glass covertly whenever the stewardess was busy supplying the coach passengers forward with balsa-wood rolls, and some gray meat that resembled cardboard left out in the rain, and whatever other delicacies they were getting for their thirty-three dollars. Mrs. Infeld could hardly help noticing my extralegal boozing, but she observed the ancient code of *omerta*.

"Do you always eat so lavish?" she finally asked me.

"Only on no-frills," I said, explaining to the best of my ability Alice's Law of Compensatory Cashflow.

"If you spent all that money on food, why didn't you go first class?" Mrs. Infeld asked.

"Because the food's no good in first class," I said.

"You're right," she said.

Mrs. Infeld seemed less suspicious after that, but a few minutes later, while I was attacking a salad of roasted peppers and eggplant that I had snared the previous evening from a restaurant in our neighborhood called Tito's, she fixed me with an accusing look and said, "You must be a gourmet eater."

I denied it, of course. The accusation made me realize, though, that I was carrying some pretty *haute* eats for a Midwestern traveling man. I explained to Mrs. Infeld that my picnic had been gathered partly by my wife, an Eastern sophisticate who knew that arugala was not a folk dance and could poach a salmon in some secret way that made it taste as good as barbecued ribs. I also pointed out that except for a mix-up the main course of my picnic would have been some cold fried chicken from another of our neighborhood restaurants, the Pink Teacup—a no-frills spot that has the look of a Harlem café transplanted to Bleecker Street as a service to Harlem expatriates and Harlem commuters in the area, the way a McDonald's or Burger King might appear off Piccadilly Circus to be of comfort to American tourists who feel the deprivation of being thousands of miles away from what they consider the real article. How could she make such an accusation, I asked, about someone who was planning to eat, as the main course of his dessert course, a delicacy that is called a Keen's Special in our neighborhood and can only be described as the final chocolate-chip cookie?

I do think Mrs. Infeld and I gradually became allies of sorts, although all I could persuade her to share with me was something that both she and I took for a deviled egg but turned out to be what a wildcat East Village caterer named Montana Palace describes, quite accurately, as "eggs stuffed with shrimp and horseradish." I don't mean she was without criticism. When I got out Montana Palace's pesto sauce and started shoveling it onto some celery, she said, "Listen, with that garlic, they're going to throw you off the plane." And she did not, I think it's fair to say, have a natural community of interest with someone who ate tomatoes stuffed with minted mussels out of a business-course briefcase. ("If you put an egg salad sandwich in front of my husband, he's happy," she said, as I was eating some pistachio pâté.) But she did not turn me in for flouting the authority of the Federal Aviation Administration, or whichever agency it is that forbids free-lance liquor on high, and she did, after all, accept from me an egg stuffed with shrimp and horseradish.

As we began our descent into Miami, I was feeling a bit like an egg stuffed with horseradish myself. I had been eating pretty steadily for an hour and a half. By prorating furiously in my head, I calculated that I had spent several dollars less on the trip than the coach passengers who were sitting only a row or two away, still looking sour from memories of the enlisted men's mess-hall rations they had suffered at the hands of the airline. I felt a bit guilty about that, so I had another piece of chocolate cake to revive my spirits.

Mrs. Infeld was telling me that her friends would never believe her. "I want you to know I had a very interesting trip," she said when we touched down. "Usually it's boring, but it wasn't boring."

"Thank you, Mrs. Infeld," I said. "It really is amazing how time passes when you keep busy."

6
Mao and Me

As long as I have decided to go along with the literary fashion of Total Disclosure, I might as well admit that my Cousin Harvey fantasy is not the only fantasy I have. For years, I have had the recurring fantasy that Mao Tse-tung makes an official visit to the United States and I am asked by the State Department to take him eating for a week in New York. The fantasy was not altered in the least by news of Mao's death. For a while, I did consider changing to the new leaders, but that possibility melted away within a few weeks of their ascension. They simply didn't strike me as either hearty eaters or cheerful dining companions; they reminded me of the dour Kremlin crowd that took over from Khrushchev and then bad-mouthed him for "phrasemongering" and other qualities I admired. I decided that for the purposes of my fantasy I would not recognize Mao's death.

That sort of thing is permitted in fantasies; Abigail and Sarah do it all the time.

Even before Mao died, I had one sticking point in my fantasy. Why would the State Department choose me instead of one of the people Alice persists in calling "grown-up food writers?" I have no influence in the State Department. Just about everyone I have ever known who entered the Foreign Service seems to have been sent immediately to Ouagadougou, Upper Volta, which, as I understand it, is not where Foreign Service officers want to be sent. Why wouldn't the wise heads at State ask, say, Craig Claiborne or Mimi Sheraton to show the Chairman around? Claiborne has co-authored a cookbook of Chinese recipes, so he might even be able to speak a couple of words of Mandarin to Chairman Mao—at least if the couple of words the Chairman wanted to hear happened to be words like "bamboo shoots" or "black mushrooms" or "hot and spicy."

Finally, after staring out of a lot of airplane windows with Mao on my mind, I invented a satisfactory reason for my receiving the assignment—an invention that permitted me to continue to what might be called the meat of the fantasy. I was specifically requested by the political officer of the Chinese delegation to the United Nations. He found me ideologically appealing. After some research, he had been able to ascertain that I was an enthusiast rather than an expert—"glutton" is a word that has occasionally been used by the unkind—and therefore a fine choice for anyone wanting to avoid the crimes of elitism or careerism or professionalism. The Chinese Cultural Revolution happens to be raging during my fantasy, and what, after all, would one call a teenage Red Guard who took over the directorship of a medical school during that period except an enthusiast rather than an expert? Asking someone like Mimi Sheraton to be the guide merely because she may know something about the subject would have made no more sense than having the former director of the medical school perform an operation merely because he happened to be a surgeon. The political officer asks the State Department for me, by name and address, adding, in slightly inexact English, "The Chairman sees with pleasure toward meeting that folk type which people in your Medium Western states are sometimes saying as a Big Hungry Boy."

Alice is, of course, appalled. The power of a fantasizer to control the fantasy may extend to reincarnating the Chairman of the Central Committee of the Communist Party of the People's Republic of China, but it falls short of being able to alter Alice's inevitable reaction to my plans for some serious eating. In my fantasy Alice had, just before the word from State came through, prevailed upon me to start a diet for which I have sworn unswerving allegiance to a peck of carrots.

"But you promised to lose ten pounds," she says, when I inform her that I've received the call.

"I wish I could keep that promise, but my country comes before any personal considerations," I say. "Think of all those people who have gone off to Ouagadougou with hardly a murmur of complaint."

"I'm afraid you're going to start looking more and more like the Chairman yourself."

"A man must do what he must do," I say.

Alice pauses for a while. "You know that Mao is the one who started calling your friend Khrushchev a phrase-monger," she finally says. This, I realize, is what the marriage counselors mean by "playing dirty." I am silent. "It was Mao who said Khrushchev was in a 'revisionist quag-mire,' " Alice continues.

"The people from State asked me not to talk politics," I say.

My Chairman Mao fantasy has to do not just with tossing aside a diet but with an old dream I have had about being able to eat a favorite dish in one restaurant and then dash off (by limousine with diplomatic license plates, if at all possible) for another favorite dish in another restaurant. It is a dining method I have always been embarrassed to employ without having the excuse of shepherding around a visiting head of state who has to sample many American dishes in the short time his busy schedule allots him. I did engage in a sort of trial run once, on a very small scale. While some friends were visiting us one day, it was decided that a friend I'll call Jones and I should pick up some food in Chinatown and bring it back to the assembled eaters. I no longer remember why we all didn't just go to Chinatown for dinner; perhaps the city was locked in a bagel-bakers' strike, making it impossible for Sarah to enter a Chinese restaurant.

On the way to Chinatown it occurred to me that there was no reason to get everything at the same restaurant. We could park the car in a strategic spot, then separate and hit two or three restaurants apiece, picking up a favorite dish in each place. In my heart of hearts, of course, I have always believed that what may actually be my favorite dish in a number of Chinatown restaurants is something I have never even had the opportunity to taste, simply because of my inability to read the wall signs that announce some house specialties in Chinese. Some time ago—many years, I should say, before such intimate family disclosures became the rage—I revealed publicly that Alice and I had been through a family disagreement concerning the signs, Alice having arbitrarily dismissed a reasonable and politely worded request that she assign some Chinese immigrant students in a class she was teaching at City College to translate the signs as a way of polishing up their English. Even without the secret dishes, though, Jones and I faced an opportunity to snatch up a spectacular variety of food within easy running distance of where we parked the car. If we planned our operation with the precision of an exquisitely plotted guerrilla raid, we could even arrive home with our booty still hot. "I don't think the flounder Fukienese style from Foo Joy will travel, so I'll grab the cold spiced kidney from Chef Ma's while you're getting the eggplant with garlic from Szechuan Cuisine," I told Jones. I hated to give up the flounder—some texture specialists of my acquaintance have rated it "eighty percent crunch"—but in these sorts of operations losses have to be cut ruthlessly and decisions made with no hesitation. If someone paused to bemoan the fact that green fish from Say Eng Look or pork dumplings from one of the *dim sum* houses might not make it from Chinatown to the Village in good order, he could ruin the entire operation. Ten minutes after Jones and I had fanned out—if two people can be said to have fanned—we were back in the car, loaded with specialties. We had taken no losses except for a slight bruise I acquired when I knocked over an elderly lady while escaping from Phoenix Garden with the Pepper and Salty Shrimp. The operation was, in other words, a remarkable success. I think it would have gone even better if Jones had not, for reasons I can't imagine, declined to make a map of the strike zone and synchronize our watches.

"I suppose your duty to your country requires you to spend a long Saturday evening with the Chairman at the Parkway," Alice is saying, with a touch of sarcasm that many people might consider inappropriate to inquiries about an act of patriotism. In my fantasy the Parkway, one of the last of the Rumanian-Jewish restaurants in New York, is still on Allen Street, on the Lower East Side; actually, it closed and then reopened again in the forties, but my fantasies have never worked well in midtown. Alice always said she was fond of the Parkway, but I sometimes thought I caught an undercurrent of disapproval—another hint that agents of the Balanced Diet Conspiracy may have been sneaking over to lobby with her whenever I left town. There is no question that Rumanian-Jewish food is heavy. One meal is equal in heaviness, I would guess, to eight or nine years of steady mung-bean eating. Following the Rumanian tradition, garlic is used in excess to keep the vampires away; following the Jewish tradition, a dispenser of schmaltz (liquid chicken fat) is kept on the table to give the vampires heartburn if they get through the garlic defense. The standard line about Rumanian-Jewish cooking is usually credited to Zero Mostel, some of whose friends remember him as a legendary New York eater who did some acting and painting on the side: "It's killed more Jews than Hitler."

"I've decided that the Parkway would not be appropriate," I say, in a tone of voice that makes it clear that sacrificing my own desires for the good of my country is for me an everyday occurrence. I have decided that during the

Chairman's visit I will forgo places that would require him
to stay for a full meal in order to savor an atmosphere that
is an important part of the experience. It would have been
impossible just to dash into the old Parkway on a Saturday
night, wolf down a plate of chopped liver with schmaltz and
chopped onion and chopped radish and greven (cracklings
from rendered chicken fat), and then dash out again. What
if the strolling accordion player happened to be playing
"Hava Nagilah" and everyone in the restaurant felt like joining in? What if Teddy Southard, known to some regulars as
"the goyishe waiter," had just reached the most dramatic
verse of "If I Loved You," which he was singing while
standing in the midde of the dining room holding an arm-
ful of dirty dishes? The goyishe waiter got his sobriquet
because of being so relentlessly gentile that at the Parkway
he stood out like John V. Lindsay at the dedication of a
Hasidic synagogue. The G. W.'s real ambition, of course,
was to be an actor, and if he had ever made it he would
have undoubtedly been typecast as a sophisticate. At the
Parkway he would set a huge bowl of mashed potatoes on the
table, hold the schmaltz above them in one hand and the
greven in the other, and say, in the tone and diction George
Sanders might have used while holding a cognac bottle
above the empty glass of a dinner guest, "May I?" The Parkway used to have another singing waiter, Murray Kaye, but
he never started a song while he was holding dishes; he
needed both hands to sing. He sometimes referred to himself as "the last of the belt-'em-out singers." I knew that the
Chairman might enjoy meeting Murray and exchanging
some showbiz stories, and he would certainly have liked to
meet the chef of the Parkway in those days—a Puerto Rican
named Florentino Salas, who, when asked once if it had

been difficult for a Puerto Rican to master Rumanian-Jewish cooking, said, "I learned from a colored fella who was here." But, knowing that stopping at the Parkway meant stopping for the entire evening, I reluctantly cut it from my list. What a man entrusted with the appetite of Chairman Mao needs, I explain to Alice, is restraint.

"In that case," she says. "They may end up with Craig Claiborne or Mimi Sheraton after all."

The Chairman has arrived. Instead of just having his chauffeur honk the limousine horn for me, he has come in to meet the entire family. Alice mumbles something to him about the role of healthy nutritional habits in building a revolutionary society, and he smiles politely. Cousin Harvey offers to put him into Costa Rican soybeans on the ground floor. Sarah, despite our entreaties, has insisted on holding a bagel while the Chairman is in the house, but he appears not to notice. "Well," I finally say cheerfully, "it's Brooklyn night tonight, Mr. Chairman." Off we go in his limousine to gobble down a Brooklyn dish here and a Brooklyn dish there.

Fifteen minutes later the limousine has pulled to a stop in front of Gage & Tollner—that testimony, in a city full of mad-dog restaurant discoverers, to the pleasures of a thoroughly discovered restaurant. "Just the soft-clam-belly appetizers here, Mr. Chairman," I say—just the bellies of succulent clams (their necks and tails having presumably been donated to *The New York Times* Hundred Neediest Cases), barely floured and broiled in butter. Almost before the waiter realizes that he has served the Chairman of the Central Committee of the Communist Party of the People's Republic of China—almost, in fact, before I have a chance to ask if it might be possible to get a bowl of Duxbury Stew to go—we are off to pick up some French fries at the original Coney Island Nathan's and stop for a steak at Peter Luger's. (Alice, having completely lost her aloofness in all the excitement of meeting the Chairman, had shouted out the window as we were leaving "Remember—foreigners love steak!") The Chairman is still nodding his pleasure at Peter Luger's tomato-and-onion salad as I lead him to the limousine that will take us to Junior's for cheesecake.

The Mao fantasy often returns, I find, when I'm doing something like standing in the kitchen munching a raw zucchini, trying to concentrate on calculating whether the difference in taste between honey-vanilla yogurt and plain yogurt is worth the difference in calories. My mind starts to wander, and I find myself putting together a peripatetic meal for the Chairman and me. We are dashing around town for Italian food—stopping in Little Italy at one place for the roast-pepper appetizer and at another for fried mixed vegetables. We cut up to the Village for pasta—splitting first some *paglia e fieno* ("No, no, the larger portion is for you, Mr. Chairman—you're the guest") and then some of Tito's cannelloni stuffed with cornmeal ("Well, thanks, Mr. Chairman—maybe just another spoonful or two"). Then we head uptown to let one of the running dogs of imperialism who operate the fancy Italian places set some veal before us (side dish of escarole for me, thanks very much) before we head right back downtown to Grand Street for a cup of cappuccino and a selection of Italian pastries. While I am enjoying a particularly delicious sfogliatelle, the Chairman's interpreter asks the waiter for a dish of plain yogurt, and the resulting ridicule forces him to wait for us in the car.

Sometimes I don't bother to organize the meal by borough or type of food; particularly when I'm in one of my raw-vegetable periods, I daydream of random dishes that have nothing in common except how much better they taste than celery. The Chairman and I stroll through the Village to the Coach House for some black bean soup—they are sticky about whether a Mao jacket is the equivalent of a coat and tie until I point out, "This is not just a Mao jacket, this is Mao"—and then rush up to Harlem to have Suzy-Q potatoes at Thomforde's. I tell the driver that he might as well take First Avenue up to Harlem so that we can stop on the way to pick up a few hedges against starving in the car— a stop at Kurowycky's butcher shop for Polish meatloaf, maybe, and a stop at the Foccaceria, which serves what some people I know call "the best spleen sandwich in the Borough of Manhattan."

"It would be out of the way to take First Avenue to Harlem," the driver says, in more or less the same tone Alice used to point out that Mrs. Palladino's restaurant was not on the way to the rain forest.

The Chairman gives him a look that has promises of fourteen years in a reeducation camp in Yunnan, and we head up First Avenue. The Chairman loves these eclectic meals. "Let a thousand dishes be served," he says.

When it is all over, Chairman Mao is exceedingly grateful, as well as a few pounds heavier. As a going-away gift, I tell him that if he drives to LaGuardia by the Williamsburg Bridge / Brooklyn-Queens Expressway route, he practically has to pass Russ & Daughters, the appetizer store of my dreams. That means he can supply himself with some Nova Scotia salmon and a pound or two of chopped herring and maybe a nice piece whitefish, then drop into Moishe's Bakery, a couple of doors away, for the kind of pumpernickel bagels not ordinarily available in Peking, and then double back to Ben's Dairy, between Russ's and Moishe's, where he can buy a baked farmer cheese with scallions that, reheated in the People's Republic, would make him think fondly of America even if, in an idle moment, our government decided to invade.

He wants to give me the Order of the People's Struggle against Reactionary Landlords, or some such. I decline, modestly. He offers me a smallish province, internationally famous for its dumplings. I tell him no reward is necessary, the pleasure having been all mine. He insists on doing something to repay me. "Well," I finally say, "if you could just lend me your interpreter for one afternoon, Mr. Chairman. There are certain wall signs in some restaurants in Chinatown I happen to be very interested in."

7
Confessions of a Crab Eater

When I read in *The New York Times* one winter that Dungeness crabs were being caught in California almost faster than they could be eaten, I didn't rush right out there the way some crazed Wedgwood collector might have dashed off to London when the pound dropped to a dollar seventy-five. I did manage, though, to make it to the West Coast on business well before the end of the season. I try to show some restraint and still get plenty to eat. On the plane to California the seat next to me—the seat I might ordinarily expect to find occupied by a regional sales manager or an itinerant shopping-center developer—was occupied instead by my own wife, Alice, who was chattering away about how beautiful the coast of Northern California must be when all the wildflowers bloom in the spring. Alice's business in Calilfornia, as far as I could gather from the conversation, was to shoot me full of scenery propaganda while I was trying my best to get something decent to eat.

Someone who has a serious interest in eating Dungeness crabs cannot dally indefinitely on the East Coast; the Dungeness is a West Coast creature, named for a small town in Washington. Even on the West Coast, someone who wants to eat a Dungeness crab that was alive and crawling twenty minutes before the meal has his work cut out for him. On either coast of the United States, a lot of fish seem to leap out of the sea straight into a flash freezer. Even fish restaurants on harbors often seem to have chosen the spot more for the ambience than the source of supply— the fish caught in the picturesque bay visible through the fishnet-covered windows having apparently found their way by truck to Boston, where they were frozen and sent back, without unseemly haste. For a long time, I have had the suspicion that Alaska and Florida are providing each other's shorefront restaurants with bland frozen fish, in the way that some countries with cultural-exchange agreements provide each other with overly polite high school students.

Alice and I once spent several days in an Alaskan seaport whose restaurants offered the traveler less chance of coming across a fresh piece of fish than he might have if he were entrapped in a farm county of Arkansas—where he might at least have the good fortune to stumble upon an only recently dispatched catfish. Alice was beginning to look desperate. I was forced to remind her that when she first expressed a longing to see the magnificent, snow-covered mountains of Alaska, I had prudently mentioned my theory that the quality of food a place offers is often in inverse proportion to the splendors of its scenery—a phenomenon I account for with the additional theory that the cooks in a spectacularly beautiful place are often outside drinking in nature's wonderments instead of standing in front of a hot stove where they belong. Alice has not had the opportunity to test out my theory thoroughly, since the business trips on which she decides I need company have never happened to be trips to middle-sized industrial cities in Ohio.

My reminder, for some reason, only made Alice look more desperate. The Alaskan seaport did have a fish plant that processed Dungeness crabs—boiling them as they came in off the boats and freezing them in brine to produce what the trade calls "brine-frozen whole cooks"—and finally I paid what I allowed myself to think of as a courtesy call on the manager.

"Nice operation you have here," I said, sidling up to one of the huge boiling pots. "A shame all of these get shipped away."

"Would you like one of these crabs?" my host said, snatching from the cooling table a crab that must have been ten inches across the shell.

I took it and ran. Back at the motel, Alice and I had already supplied ourselves with Portuguese wine and Hydrox cookies—the pick of the provisions in that seaport. I spread a newspaper on the floor to prepare the main course, only to discover that the crepe-soled shoes I was wearing were totally useless for cracking a crab shell. Fortunately, Alice had some sturdy wooden heels, which did the trick, and we settled down to the best meal we had in Alaska. "Alice," I said, when we had polished off about half the crab, "I'm certainly glad you decided to come along."

The fact that I would go to some trouble to get my hands on a Dungeness crab—the fact that I would do a little polite panhandling in Alaska, or even transport myself to California with barely seemly haste—does not mean that I prefer Dungeness crabs to all others. In New Orelans one of our favorite pastimes is eating in lakefront restaurants where boiled shellfish are served up on beer trays and the only problem left in life is whether to attack the crabs or the boiled shrimp first. I have spent some happy evenings in Baltimore in one of those restaurants where all that seems required for happiness is a pile of Maryland blue crabs on a piece of butcher paper and a wooden mallet and a supply of napkins. (My only regret about eating crabs in Baltimore is that the crab restaurants don't serve my favorite local side order, deep-fried potato skins—a dish that is available, as far as I know, only in a flashy joint otherwise notable only for the shine on the shoes of its headwaiter. If only the Chairman were here, I sometimes muse when I have time for only one meal in Baltimore. I do manage to down a few crabs while I try to come up with a plausible geopolitical reason for a Chinese head of state to be visiting Baltimore.) Driving through the wheat fields of Kansas or the mountains of eastern Kentucky, I have found myself daydreaming of the cracked-crab salad at Mosca's outside New Orleans, or of she-crab soup at Henry's, across from the city market in Charleston, South Carolina. The mixed blessing of an American city's maintaining a cultural identity is expressed for me in the question of whether I would be willing to endure a lecture on the authenticity of detail in the historical renovation of Charleston south of Broad Street if I were allowed to eat Charleston she-crab soup while I listened.

In a fishing town near the California-Oregon state line, where Alice and I once stopped for a quick bite on her way to the scenic wonders of the Oregon coastline and my way to a renowned seafood restaurant in Newport called Mo's, I ate something called a crab-burger—openly, in full view of the other diners—and I loved it. It was not as good as a Maryland crab cake served on the Eastern shore at some place like Pope's Tavern, in Oxford, but then, hardly anything is. For me, the coming of spring has nothing to do with the appearance of crocuses or robins; spring is here when soft-shell crabs begin appearing on the menus of fish houses and West Side French bistros in Manhattan. When I am in Florida, I search out a stone-crab palace and tell my dining companions to quit comparing stone crabs unfavorably with blue crabs or favorably with lobsters and just enjoy themselves. When I'm in New York, I go regularly to some place like the Yun Luck Rice Shoppe in Chinatown for crab Cantonese style—cooked in the shell with scallions and pork and ginger, and served with a selection of hand-wiping supplies. When I'm in England, I search out the sort of crabs that are cooked on boats in the North Sea and then sold in open markets. When it comes to crabs, I'm ecumenical.

My fondness for crabs may have something to do with having suffered a crab-deprived childhood. The largest body of water near Kansas City is Lake Lotawana, a lake so small that it is said to rise a foot and a half on Fourth of July weekend, when everyone gets in at once. There are people who claim that the way boats are anchored in Lake Lotawana is to lay them across the lake, like a butterknife. When I first met Alice, I was trying to impress her, of course, and, not wanting her to think me an inlander completely ignorant of sophisticated eats, I told her that Lotawana had a species of lake crab that was remarkable for the delicacy of its taste. Then one day I told her about how I used to go down to the lake before dawn when I was a boy to buy crabs right off the boats and then sit around swapping tales with the old freshes who always hung around the dock.

"Old freshes?" she said.

"Yeah, like old salts," I said. "Only fresh water."

"I don't believe old freshes," she said. "When it gets right down to it, I don't believe lake crabs."

I'm still trying to impress her. I am not always successful, of course, but the story making the rounds that I still have to have her extract the heart of my artichoke for me is completely untrue. She does sometimes extract the heart of my artichoke for me, but strictly on a volunteer basis.

"It was because of the crab that the Wharf became so popular," the guidebook in our San Francisco hotel room said of Fisherman's Wharf. "It is one of the world's most delectable catches, one of the most remembered treats of San Francisco. Descendants of the Italian fishermen who first cast nets into the seas off San Francisco in the 1850's began to line the Wharf with huge iron pots, cooking live crabs and selling them to passers-by." The huge iron pots were still there. So, of course, were the passers-by—so many that we had difficulty passing by them on the way to the crab pots. "Dungeness-deprived couple!" I wanted to shout. "Desperate Easterners! Let 'em through, folks!"

We finally made it to a crab boiler, a cheerful fellow who once ran a small seafood restaurant just on the other side of the walkway from his crab pot but had finally decided to turn the restaurant into a souvenir stand. ("This way, you don't have to worry all the time about the clam chowder spoiling.") While we were waiting for our crab to boil, he informed me that this most remembered treat of San Francisco had been trucked in the night before from Eureka, two hundred and forty miles up the coast. The fishermen who were going out of Eureka and Crescent City for crabs may have been having a spectacular year, but San Francisco fishermen hadn't been able to catch enough crabs to supply even the Fisherman's Wharf crab pots for more than the first two or three weeks of the season. The crab hawkers on the Wharf were in the position of country farm-stand operators who, having sold off too much of the farm for real-estate developments, find themselves importing fruits and vegetables from the city market in order to supply the summer people.

For reasons that are not certain to anyone, the supply of Dungeness crabs off the West Coast of the United States rises and falls dramatically in cycles of about eight to ten years. In the early sixties, though, the catch in central California—the vicinity of San Francisco Bay, which has historically acted as a nursery for crabs—leveled off, so that the low end of the cycle became a dismal norm. I suspect there are people in California who are quite certain that San Francisco had its crab supply shut off for more or less the same reason that Sodom and Gomorrah encountered their difficulties, but I learned that the Calilfornia Department of Fish and Game had been investigating other possibilities. As soon as I felt full enough to travel, we drove from San Francisco to Menlo Park to talk with Dr. Harold Orcutt, the director of the fish and game department's crab project. Alice said she wanted to meet Orcutt because of her interest in scientific matters—she happens to be the one in our family who reads books about brain research and puts together the stereo—but I suspected that her interest had something to do with rumors that a restaurant in

Princeton, California, more or less on the way to Menlo Park, served fresh abalone.

Alice has a weakness for abalone, and, being a husband who does his best to anticipate even her unexpressed desires, I try to eat as much of it with her as possible. Abalone may be the one indestructible shellfish. Canned crabmeat tastes like Styrofoam. A bad version of she-crab soup in Charleston tastes like the sauce used on lobster Newburg by the third fanciest French restaurant in Tulsa. The sort of shrimp hidden under a pound and a half of batter on what Midwestern menus call "French-fried butterfly shrimp" could as easily be turnips. Abalone seems to defy efforts to gussy it up. At Lazio's, a restaurant attached to a fish plant in Eureka, I once ordered something called Scalone— despite the fact that it sounded more like the Water Commissioner of Hoboken than something to eat—and what arrived, a sort of patty made out of abalone and scallops, was delicious.

Abalone is difficult to find in California these days. The shortage, according to one theory, may have something to do with efforts in recent years to preserve the sea otter, that cute little creature that tourists like to observe as it perches on rocks just off high-priced beach-fronts and cleverly opens shellfish—shellfish that happen to be abalone. I have nothing against sea otters—we have what might be considered a shared interest or a community of taste—but I'm not certain that the lobby organized for their protection was aware of quite how much of what those adorable creatures were getting down. It's all a matter of priorities, I suppose, and mine have something to do with the fact that when someone mentions the delights of observing creatures use their manual dexterity to open shellfish, the creatures that leap to my mind are not sea otters off the beach in Monterey but oyster shuckers at the Acme in New Orleans.

Having filled ourselves with abalone, we searched out Dr. Orcutt, who turned out to be a man who spoke with the traditional detachment of a scientist unless he happened to be on the subject of eating blue crabs on the East Coast as a boy. Orcutt emphasized that he and his fellow researchers were still a long way from accumulating enough data to discover precisely what was causing the dearth of crabs in the waters outside of San Francisco Bay. They may never know. Scientists are still not certain why the sardines that used to be so prevalent around the same area were some years ago replaced by anchovies; it may even be that the sardines existed in such profusion for what seemed like so many years merely because of some temporary imbalance in the ecological system, and that everything has now returned to normal. I have always thought of sardines as more normal than anchovies myself, but, my understanding of such matters being so primitive that I spent an embarrassing number of years in the belief that marshmallows grew on bushes, I decided not to offer that opinion to Dr. Orcutt as something he might want to pass along to the sardines-and-anchovies crowd.

Orcutt's project was working on the theory that any one of several factors could have crippled the crab crop—some natural environmental variation, such as a change in water temperature, or man-made pollution in San Francisco Bay, or fishing pressure, or some combination of factors that reduced the crab stock below the level at which it could "snap back" from the low end of the cycle. Orcutt was certain of the answer to one question I had—why crabmeat that has been out of the shell for a while tends to taste like chopped balsa wood. Exposure to the air, he said, oxidizes the crab's natural fats, and the fats are the source of the crab's flavor. The scientifically correct complaint to make when served tasteless crab in a restaurant is, I now know, "Waiter, this crab's natural fats must have been oxidizing since last Tuesday."

The fishermen who hang around Fisherman's Wharf were not as cautious as Orcutt about explaining why the crabs have disappeared. A fisherman asked about an unnatural absence of fish tends to speak with the assurance of an orthopedist who has been hired as an expert witness in a negligence case—and like the orthopedist, he is not troubled by hearing a colleague present conflicting testimony with equal authority. We found fishermen who believed that the crabs were destroyed because cities were dumping their garbage into the ocean, and we found fishermen who believed that the crabs were destroyed because some fools forced the cities to stop dumping garbage into the ocean, thus depriving the young crabs of food. There were a lot of fishermen who believed the problem was caused by the dumping of industrial wastes into San Francisco Bay. There were fishermen who believed that the crab drought, like a lot of other problems, can be traced to Russian trawlers. According to a fish processor I spoke with in Eureka, the Russians may have actually helped the crab supply there by taking a lot of hake, which feed on baby crabs, but that is not a theory I heard from fishermen. Before the United States declared a two-hundred-mile limit, American fishermen tended to resent the Russians not only for where they fished but for how they fished—from huge trawlers that are to the average American fishing boat what the largest supermarket in Orange County is to a mom-and-pop corner store. A group of American fishermen standing around a wharf are more likely to drop a kind word about gale-force winds than about the Russians.

Fisherman's Wharf puts less emphasis on the edible part of a shellfish than on the ashtrays or hula dolls that can be made out of its shell. After walking through the souvenir stands on the Wharf, it is rather astonishing to turn the corner and suddenly come upon fishing boats—real fishing boats, with names like Skip-A-Lou and Baby Carl. The effect is the same as traveling through the Pennsylvania Dutch country, amid manufactured hex signs and plastic horse-and-buggy reproductions and placemats with bad jokes written phonetically in a vaudeville Pennsylvania Dutch dialect, and coming across an Amishman riding down the road in a buggy that looks just like the miniature buggies in the gift shop. It is something of a shock to realize that the Pennsylvania Dutch actually exist, living there in the same area that sells pictures of them on ashtrays. The fishing boats Alice and I saw at Fisherman's Wharf were not, of course, the source of the crabs we saw being cooked in the huge crab pots. The signs that said FRESH LOCAL CRAB were completely accurate only if Eureka is taken to be in the Greater San Francisco area. But the crabs were, in fact, the freshest that could be found in San Francisco; the trucks being sent every night from Eureka specifically serviced the crab stalls and the relatively few restaurants in town that are particular about freshness. The best way to eat Dungeness crabs in San Francisco is still to witness your fresh crab being dropped into boiling water by one of the Wharf's crab hawkers, dash a block or two down the Embarcadero to Boudine's Bakery three minutes before the crab is done, buy a loaf of sourdough bread just out of the oven, return on the dead run to the crab pot carrying a loaf of bread that is still hot, ask the hawker to crack the crab's shell ever so slightly, and adjourn to a bench overlooking the fishing boats.

Not many tourists do that; it's too much trouble, and it's too messy. Tolerance of messiness, of course, is based partly on familiarity with the mess; there are undoubtedly Midwestern tourists on Fisherman's Wharf who would think nothing of being up to their elbows in fried chicken or barbecued ribs but recoil at taking apart a Dungeness crab. The most popular item offered by the crab hawkers is not freshly boiled crab but something called a Walk Away Cocktail—crabmeat taken from the shell early in the morning, put into a small paper cup, and kept on ice while its natural fats, I now know, are oxidized like crazy. Alice tried a Walk Away Cocktail, and took on the expression she sometimes has when Abigail and Sarah ask for more ketchup to pour on their frozen fish sticks. A Walk Away Cocktail is also available with equally tasteless shrimp instead of crab, or a combination of shrimp and crab. Eating a combination shrimp-crab Walk Away Cocktail has all the excitement of eating bologna between two different brands of packaged white bread. It is not, however, messy.

If a research team systematically interviewed serious shellfish eaters about their most memorable shellfish experience, I suspect that the unifying theme of the testimony would be messiness. Ask anyone who truly loves shellfish about the best he has ever had, and the answer tends to be a story ending with the table being hosed down after the meal or mountains of shells being shoveled into trash bins. It is apparent to serious shellfish eaters that in the great evolutionary scheme of things crustaceans developed shells to protect them from knives and forks. Extracting fish from a shell tends to be time-consuming, but shellfish eaters are, as a group, patient. In fact, the most pedantic among them— those amateur professors of shelling who loiter around Chesapeake Bay—sometimes seem more interested in extracting crabmeat with finesse than in eating it.

American restaurants operate on the premise that most of their customers do not want to engage in that sort of dirty work just to get at food they are paying good money for. Tarantino's restaurant on Fisherman's Wharf has on its menu something called Lazy Man's Cioppino, described as "Famous local shellfish stew of the native fisherman. Prawns, clams, crabs, eastern oysters—with all the meat removed from the shell." I suspect that the popularity in America of frozen South African lobster tails can be accounted for by their being so easy to eat—the only other logical explanation being that Americans, for some reason, are attracted to the taste of unpainted papier-mâché if it is priced high enough.

To a restaurant proprietor, a customer who eats a simple dish with dispatch is a customer who is likely to turn the table over to another customer rather quickly. Even one of those East Side New York steak restaurants that bully the innocent into paying twenty-three dollars for a lobster would probably lose money on the most thorough lobster eater I know—a friend of ours in Nova Scotia named Russell Harnish—because of how long he would keep the table tied up while he was doing justice to the lobster. Russell is a methodical man. He takes a lobster apart the way a senior infantry sergeant disassembles an exceedingly complicated machine gun, and when he finishes his meal the lobster looks as though it might have been staked out on an anthill for a couple of weeks. I suppose that in the time it takes Russell Harnish to eat one lobster McDonald's sells twenty or thirty million hamburgers.

When we eat lobster with Russell Harnish, Alice spends a lot of time studying him, the way an apprentice silversmith might watch a master turn out a particularly difficult bowl. Alice is a practiced dismantler of lobsters herself, although the story making the rounds that she still has to show me how to break off the claws happens to be what the politicians call "untrue and completely out of context." It is generally true, though, that even after years of living in New York the two mysteries of the East that remain beyond the reach of an expatriate Midwesterner are the New York subway system and the proper eating of a lobster. Someone who comes to lobster eating or subway transportation late faces the sort of frustrations faced by someone who applies himself diligently to studying French with the realization that no matter how many hours he spends in the language lab there are thousands of words like "diaper pin" and "ball bearing" he will probably never know. We inlanders sometimes imagine we have conquered the subway, but our conquest, upon close examination by a native, usually consists of nothing more than some straight shots on the West Side I.R.T. or some rather clumsy combination put together with the Forty-second Street shuttle. There are out-of-towners who have cornered the market in one thing or another in Wall Street and there are out-of-towners who command attention at Sardi's, but I have never met an out-of-towner who has broken the code of the B. M. T. We remain equally ignorant of the final mysteries of lobster dismemberment. But, the taste of a lobster not being a taste that has to be acquired, we wade right in, like cheerful hackers who have a fine time on the course while shooting a sixty-four for nine holes.

8
Dinner with Friends

When we're dressing to go to someone's house for dinner, Alice often tries to persuade me that there are ways of showing appreciation to the hostess other than having thirds. I suppose there are ways of displaying appreciation for an artist's painting other than writing out a check on the spot and snatching the painting from the wall, but is "My, how interesting" really what he wants to hear? There cannot be many cooks so confident in their skill that the possibility of their having, say, put too much salt in the soup does not occur to them when a dinner guest says, "Thanks, it was delicious but I couldn't eat another bite" or "I'm saving room for dessert."

"They know I can eat another bite, Alice," I try to explain, hoping that she has not noticed that I am having some mild difficulty getting my collar buttoned. "And how can I tell them I'm saving room for dessert when it is widely known that my policy with food is to eat it on a first-come-first-served basis?"

"It wouldn't hurt not to live up to your reputation one night," Alice says. "In fact, it wouldn't hurt to change your reputation."

"My mother told me always to be polite," I reply weakly.

When I'm on the road and someone asks me to dinner, I am sometimes able to phone Alice late in the evening to report that I have displayed the sort of restraint she so admires. There is some food that inspires abstemiousness even in me. Naturally, I try to avoid exposing myself to it. When someone I have met in another city suggests that I "come on out to the house" that evening, I believe I owe it to myself to try to figure out, as politely as possible, whether he is married to someone who is always pouring canned mushroom soup all over everything. A traveling man can't be to careful. I stall the invitation with some talk about whether my work will be finished by dinner time, and then I try to feel around for what the percentages are of getting a better meal than I might find trying to sniff out a barbecue joint that uses real hickory wood or a Mexican restaurant that serves tripe. (I don't particularly like tripe, but, after many years of research, I have finally decided that its presence on the menu of a Mexican restaurant is a badge representing seriousness of intention.) Anybody who finds this approach to a dinner invitation callous or cynical or lacking in graciousness has not spent much time on the road.

"Where did you and your wife meet?" I might say to some politician in Toledo, supposedly making idle conversation but actually hoping against hope for the long shot that he took a war bride from an Italian village known throughout Europe for the perfection of its gnocchi. Or, speaking to a newspaperman in Cedar Rapids, I might say, "I guess the corn is pretty good out this way"—waiting to see if his response is an uninterested grunt or the information that he always waits until dinner is precisely three and a half minutes away before snapping a few cobs off the stalks in his backyard and passing them to his son, who is faster at short distances, to shuck as he proceeds at a dead run to the pot of boiling water waiting on the stove.

Now and then I am simply lucky. In Vermont once, having taken a wild guess that the couple in question might be the sort of people who would make the best use of what the land around them provided, I accepted a dinner invitation with a haste that Alice might have considered unseemly and was rewarded with a dinner that included a dish, made from apples and coarse maple syrup, that was probably the best dessert I have ever eaten. In El Paso, during a particularly bitter clothing-workers' strike, I was asked by a priest known for his support of the strikers whether I might like to stay for a bowl of chili verde. The priest seemed to me to have demonstrated the sort of attention to detail often found in gifted cooks: when the company being struck ran a full-page newspaper advertisement that listed eight thousand "happy workers"—people who immediately became known as "happies"—the priest, with a patience that I have always associated with seminaries, counted the names and found 2,329. It also happens that I have never eaten a bowl of chili verde I didn't like. The chili verde was magnificent —the masterpiece, as I learned later, not of the priest but of a local woman who had a singularly delicious way of demonstrating her devotion to the parish.

The staggering apple-and-syrup dessert and the magnificent chili verde are memorable exceptions to a body of experience that runs more in the direction of canned mushroom soup. I may run across the Italian war bride in Toledo and then find out that nothing makes her feel more American than being able to serve frozen food right out of the package—an announcement she makes while I am shoving Sarah's favorite brand of fish sticks from one part of my plate to another. I fall for a young executive's eloquent declamation about the wonders of his wife's cooking, and discover, once it is much too late, that I am eating a dinner prepared by the St. Paul or Denver or Moline version of the newlywed gourmet-food mongers we used to refer to in New York as "the beef Stroganoff crowd."

"My, how interesting," I say to the hostess, while silently comforting myself with the reminder that I can at least look forward to beginning my telephone conversation with Alice that night by saying, "Alice, you would have really been proud of me this evening. A man with real will power is a pleasure to behold."

One evening, after we returned home from a dinner during which I had managed to do the sort of eating that compliments the hostess on her cooking and takes care of any left-over glut at the same time, Alice tried the sympathetic approach. "I suppose one of the problems is that too many people we know are good cooks," she said.

"That is not my idea of a problem, Alice," I said. "In fact, compared to, say, the problem of spiraling world-wide inflation or the energy problem or the race problem in South Africa, it doesn't seem like a problem at all." Alice has not spent much time on the road herself.

In a way, of course, she was right. A lot of people we know in New York serve dinners that demand gestures of appreciation—sometimes two or three gestures, if there seems to be enough in the pot. Some of the people, I suppose, are reformed members of the beef Stroganoff crowd. Some of them went through a period of ingredient purity during which dinner conversations were so dominated by talk of how to prepare stone-ground flour or where to buy the true fig that I found myself imagining a cook pure enough to grind her own cleanser. Then, before all the talk of authenticity and purity could have any serious effect on my appetite, the period was passed, and so were the seconds.

One New York cook we know who never seemed to go through any of the unfortunate phases is a friend of ours named Colette Rossant, whose dinner invitations I have always treated the way a Savings and Loan lobbyist might treat a note asking him to a small poker game with the members of the Senate Banking Committee. Colette is French, and had had no trouble at all remaining so in the South Village, which everybody else thinks is an Italian neighborhood. The Italian coteghino sausage she buys from Mrs. Canevari on Sullivan Street is somehow transformed into extremely French *saucisson en croûte* by being carried a few hundred yards into her kitchen. She does her shopping daily, like any French housewife, and if she finds a loaf of bread not quite as fresh as she expects it to be, she does not hesitate to bring the matter up with the man who baked it. I have occasionally tried to envision what must happen among the shopkeepers of the South Village when Colette Rossant, the Scourge of Sullivan Street, starts out with her shopping bag over her arm. "She's coming! The lady's coming!" the butcher must shout, spotting her from the doorway as he sweeps out the store. The baker rushes over to snatch away the day-old bread he had slid onto the top of the bread pile for the unsuspecting. The fruit and vegetable men begin to police their orange displays and squeeze the wilted leaves off the outside of their lettuce. Unlike the Italian war bride in Toledo whose dinner table I dread, Colette defies Americanization. She is so far above frozen food that I have always suspected she may not keep ice cubes. The Rossants live within walking distance of our house, and Alice claims that when we are walking there for dinner she is often forced to grab me by the jacket two or three times to keep me from breaking into a steady, uncharacteristic trot.

Sullivan Street is the scene every June of the Feast of St. Anthony, an Italian street fair I happen to love. (I happen to love all Italian street fairs. In fact, I even love Armenian street fairs: the One World Festival held every fall by the St. Vartan Cathedral is one of my favorite annual events.) Lately the Italians who run St. Anthony's have been permitting some foreign-food booths to creep in. Unlike the Armenians, though—whose commitment to One World is so strong that Philippine bean-sprout fritters and even Tibetan dumplings are permitted right next to the stuffed grape leaves—the Italians keep the outlanders so far south of Houston Street, where almost all fairgoers start their eating, that few people could possibly make it to the Korean egg rolls or the Greek spinach pie without being so stuffed with sausage sandwiches and calzone and clams and pasta that they can only stare numbly at the souvlaki signs. One year, in the foreign ghetto, we noticed two teenage girls operating a booth whose sign said, of all things, "Crêpes suzettes."

"Crêpes suzettes!" Alice said. "At St. Anthony's!"

The girls, of course, turned out to be Rossant daughters —like their mother, unreconstructed.

Once, a few days before we were due at the Rossants' for what Colette had promised to be a particularly worthwhile feast—the preparations for which, I assumed, had tradesmen as far uptown as Fourteenth Street quivering at their counters—I felt a cold coming on.

"A cold!" I said to Alice. "This is a disaster!"

"Are we comparing it now to spiraling world-wide inflation?"

"This is nothing to joke about, Alice," I said. "You know I always lose my sense of taste at some point during a cold."

As the evening approached, my taste buds seemed to wither away. While Alice was dressing for dinner, I was still desperately alternating wild gargling and nose-blowing in an effort to clear some taste. As soon as we walked in, I picked up a couple of pieces of celery from a bowl of *crudités* that Colette had put out with drinks. I could taste nothing. I staved off a serious depression by telling myself that celery doesn't have much taste anyway. Then I tried some coteghino. Nothing. A man who cannot taste Mrs. Canevari's coteghino cannot taste. I spent the rest of the evening trying to imagine, by texture and by the blissful looks on the faces of the other diners, what the food I was eating tasted like.

"What sin did I commit to deserve this?" I asked Alice when we got home.

"If I had to guess, I'd guess gluttony," Alice said.

An hour after we had gone to sleep, I woke up coughing. "Go take some cough medicine," Alice mumbled.

"I don't have any cough medicine."

"There's some of Abigail's in the medicine cabinet,"

Alice said. "Red. Be careful not to take the other red stuff —it's to make kids throw up if they eat something dangerous."

I stumbled off, and came back to bed. Ten minutes later, I sat straight up in bed, possessed by a wave of nausea.

"Oh, you haven't—" Alice said. But by the speed with which I was making for the bathroom, she knew I had.

Moments later, I understood for the first time how those characters in Sholom Aleichem stories can find themselves talking personally to the Divinity. "There must have been some misunderstanding, Lord," I said, when I was able to talk. "I didn't even taste it in the first place."

9
British Boiled

"Don't you miss England?" Alice, the family intellectual and crypto-travel-agent, asked me one winter. "If we flew from Halifax, we'd have all the money we saved by not flying all the way from New York, so we'd have money left over."

"I suppose we could use the surplus to endow a chair of economics somewhere," I said.

It was rather late in the year for Alice to be making summer travel plans. Usually, she likes to have them in the ground by the autumnal equinox. I knew she was itching to go somewhere. A few years before, a bizarre plan we had concocted for a cut-rate trip to China had fallen through— it entailed joining an organization in Kansas City that I remember as the Cricket Camera Club—and not taking a trip to China is, according to Alice's Law of Compensatory Cash Flow, the equivalent of a small killing in the New York State Lottery.

I don't mean that Alice is the only one in our family who likes to travel. I go along cheerfully, even though I spend so much of my time in hotels during the year on business that I can sometimes feel like Eloise all grown up. When I can't seem to find the key to my own house, it occasionally occurs to me that I may have absent-mindedly dropped it into a mailbox, postage presumably guaranteed by Abigail and Sarah.

"England is not a bad idea," I said to Alice. "The potato latkes are dynamite."

"Is that what comes to your mind when you think about England?" Alice asked.

The potato latkes were definitely in my mind. I could see myself on Wentworth Street in the East End of London. It was Sunday morning. We had just come from picking our way through Cheshire Street, where an acquisitive tourist can obtain such national treasures as a pair of fatigues from the Suez campaign. I was standing at the counter of a store called M. Marks, ordering a hot, thick potato pancake that is served on a piece of waxed paper and is eaten while standing up—a method that gives the eater the additional pleasure of being able to jump up and down occasionally in delight.

"That's amazing," Alice said.

"You're right," I said. It was amazing. England's reputation for such food is so low that a foreign correspondent of our acquaintance who was posted to London some years later—a ferocious eater I'll call Charlie Plum—arranged to have shipped from the United States among his belongings not just four bottles of Arthur Bryant's barbecue sauce and several jars of crunchy peanut butter but also an entire case of kosher dills. Plum is an awesomely energetic ferreter-out of facts, but how would anybody know that right there among people who don't even know how to spell bagel—they spell it beigel, which, oddly enough, is the way they pronounce it—a wayfarer can purchase the single best stand-up potato latke in the English-speaking world.

"When most people think of England, they think of the changing of the guard or the British Museum or sheep grazing in the English countryside or men in bowler hats going to their clubs," Alice said.

"I can do without mutton, thanks, and club food stinks," I said. "Everybody knows that." There are a number of theories to account for the failure of English club food to taste like anything at all—nostalgia for public school dining rooms and regimental mess halls, for instance—but I have always assumed that the phenomenon can be traced to a strong subconscious Anglo-Saxon belief that the tastiness of the food varies in inverse proportion to social position. The belief arrived on the East Coast of the United States from England intact with the early settlers; to this day, anyone obligated to attend a wedding at the most exclusive Long Island clubs has to make do with what tastes like Kraft Velveeta cheese sandwiches on Wonder bread (quartered and decrusted for a touch of class) and the sort of chicken à la king that brings groans from the regulars when it turns up at small-town Kiwanis luncheons.

I did have fond memories, though, that made me miss England as much as Alice did—memories that went beyond potato latkes, mostly in the direction of Chinese food. I know there is a widespread feeling that anyone with my priorities should look upon Great Britain more or less the way Charles de Gaulle used to—from a distance and down the nose. It is undoubtedly true that the English serve a number of dishes that can turn a serious eater pale—thrown into a mild state of shock by the thought that human beings have been existing on such substances for generations. (I have always been impressed, though, by how conscientious the English are about clearly labeling some of their most gruesome dishes, the way they might label dangerous medicine or a large hole in the pavement. It seems to me, for instance, that anyone who orders something called "meat and veggies" or "spotted dog" gets what he deserves. On the other hand, I must admit that in a North Carolina barbecue restaurant once, I myself ordered something called "a bag of skins," and was briefly irritated to discover that what came tasted very much like a carefully barbecued volleyball.) It does seem almost willful that at breakfast—the one meal at which an innocent traveler even in a provincial hotel has a good chance of tasting some good kippers and fresh eggs—the English refuse to serve toast until it has been hung out to dry, as if it were a pile of soggy linen.

It is also true that English food is no longer the only kind of food to be avoided in England. In recent years the place has become pockmarked with the kind of American hamburger joints that have cutesy names and less than adorable beef. The Continental Cuisine palaces in England can be even more dangerous, since they tend to be as bloated with unjustified pretense as their American counterparts—those revolving domes on the top of Midwestern bank buildings that feature Sigma Chi sommeliers and three-paragraph descriptions of which canned vegetables are going to be poured over what type of frozen sole. The English style of

Continental Cuisine was planted, I've always thought, by some Anglophobic Frenchman who managed to persuade dozens of prospective restaurant proprietors and country-hotel keepers that the way to prepare sophisticated food was to stuff something with something—almost anything—else, and then to obscure the scene of the crime with a heavy, lava-like sauce. He demonstrated to all of them, for instance, how to stuff a chicken breast with a plum that is, in turn, stuffed with an almond. I wouldn't be surprised to hear that he is now experimenting with hypodermic needles to perfect a method of stuffing the almond with paté. Since the dishes that result from these acts of cumulative stuffing all taste and weigh more or less the same, Alice and I have always referred to them by a single generic name—Stuff-Stuff with Heavy.

Eating a meal in a Stuff-Stuff with Heavy joint in the company of English people who think of themselves as gourmets is like taking a final examination in a course you hadn't meant to sign up for in the first place. Is the wine appropriate? Are there enough forks? Are there enough waiters? Did the waiter flick the crumbs from the table on the proper side of the person who deposited them there?

Once, in a Stuff-Stuff with Heavy restaurant in Bath, I happened to notice a waiter passing with a platterful of potatoes that looked superior to the sort I was eating—my habit of keeping my eyes open for a chance to covet my neighbor's side dishes having remained unbroken even in the face of occasional warnings by Alice that a man who spends as much time as I do glancing around during a meal stands the risk of dropping most of it on his lap. Naturally, I asked the waiter for a bowl or two of what he was carrying, and, having been searching for a good opportunity to take advantage of a favorable rate of exchange on the pound, I offered to bear the cost personally.

"But these are Lyonnaise potatoes," he said. "They don't go with trout."

"Never?"

"Oh no, sir," he said.

"I think I'll have some anyway," I said. He looked uncertain as to whether he wanted to be in the role of accessory in the atrocity I was about to commit. I began to feel rather uncertain myself. There was always the possibility that the waiter was a moonlighting biochemist who knew that trout and Lyonnaise potatoes produce a nearly always fatal chemical reaction if they meet in the upper colon.

Alice gave the waiter one of the smiles she reserves for assuring strangers that I am not lunatic in any dangerous way, and he gave me the potatoes—which, of course, turned out to be inferior to the ones I had been eating.

There would be no reason, though, for us to subject ourselves to any more Stuff-Stuff with Heavy joints. We could spend some time in Somerset, frying hog's pudding to a crisp and making fun of Jeffrey's eggs while gobbling up the soufflés Francie made out of them. I had no reason to be concerned about the possibility of our being dragged into any gentlemen's clubs in London. Alice and I have only one close friend who belongs to a London gentlemen's club, and we have what amounts to an understanding with him about it: we agree not to ridicule him for belonging to such an institution and he agrees not to take us there to dinner. We break our part of the agreement regularly, but he, being a gentleman, has been scrupulous about keeping his. I began to think not of what had to be avoided but of what could be savored. A satisfied look came across my face. "Yes, let's go to England this summer," I said.

"Are you really going to England just because you want a potato latke?" Alice asked.

"Of course not," I said, rather hurt. "You must think me a narrow fellow indeed. As it happens, I have just remembered the Great Dried Beef in the Sky we used to eat at the Chinese restaurant across from the Golder's Green tube stop."

When I arrived in Golder's Green one day in the middle sixties to meet an émigré politician for lunch, he said the neighborhood offered us a choice of eating at an English restaurant or a Chinese restaurant.

"May all the decisions you have to make in your political career be as simple as that one," I said.

I have been going to the Chinese restaurant across from the Golder's Green tube stop ever since. It has turned out, though, that the dishes I was so happy to find when I ate with the politician are available in a number of Peking-style restaurants in London, and that my favorite dish is no longer the dish we have always called the Great Dried Beef in the Sky (hidden behind some name like Beef with Chili Sauce on the menu) but fried seaweed, which tastes more like fried than seaweed and is worth a trip across the Atlantic on foot. England being the sort of place that encourages traditions, our family has developed a tradition of spending our first evening in London at the Chinese restaurant across from the Golder's Green tube stop, even if Sarah has not even had enough time to acquire a beigel.

My strategy for eating in London was clear from the start: eat plenty of fried seaweed and dumplings and crispy duck and crab-with-ginger and dried beef and honey-apples at Chinese restaurants. Go regularly to first-rate Indian restaurants, which are almost as difficult to find in America as fried seaweed. Eat fish—whitebait or lemon sole or turbot served in some simple fish house, like the downstairs of Manzi's, instead of in one of those fish restaurants that seem to have contracted for a steady supply of Heavy from the Stuff-Stuff with Heavy joints. Find some decent pub food or consume two or three hundred pints of ale trying. Start each and every Sunday with a stand-up potato latke on Wentworth Street.

Even before we left for England, I recognized a couple of potential difficulties in the plan. The fish house would present no problem. London has fish restaurants that are very much like serious fish houses in America. Serious fish restaurants anywhere tend to be plain rooms staffed with the sort of waiters who nod silently as they take your order, and who probably seem so much alike because they come from the same village in Italy. (The exception is in San Francisco, where the city's two serious fish houses, Sam's Grill and Tadich Grill, are staffed with Dalmatians rather than Italians—the phenomenon I always assume San Francisco boosters have in mind when they say that their city is uniquely cosmopolitan.) But I have never had much luck turning up good pub food, despite such a strong inclination to give it the benefit of the doubt that I have occasionally found myself praising pub sausages for keeping their meat content low enough to guard against heartburn. There would also be a problem, I knew, with Alice's lack of enthusiasm for Indian food. On one trip to England, she had informed me—rather bluntly, I thought, after all these years—that she believed one Indian meal every week was quite enough for her.

"I don't suppose Ceylonese and Pakistani count as Indian," I said, hoping to salvage a little something.

"It all tastes the same," Alice said.

"Surely, the nations of the Third World, aspiring to their own distinct national identity—"

"Once a week," Alice said.

My plan for getting Alice in a receptive mood for Indian food included taking her for a couple of cream teas in the country and bringing her a box of chocolate truffles from a candy store in London called Prestat—Prestat truffles being what Alice is really thinking about when she pretends to be thinking about sheep grazing in the countryside and the changing of the guard. Alice's moderation evaporates upon exposure to chocolate. I have been with her when she insists that the Trattoria, an otherwise undistinguished Italian restaurant in the Pan Am building that has by far the best chocolate ice cream in New York, is "right on the way" from Chinatown to the Village. Her discussions on the variety of chocolate cake available in our neighborhood are so erudite that I would not be surprised to read someday that she was leading a symposium on that subject at the New School. The only commerical venture I ever heard her discuss with any enthusiasm at all was a store that she and another chocophiliac we know were going to start called the Chocolate Freak. When Alice's thoughts wander from chocolate in England, she does not begin thinking about the British Museum. She begins thinking about a bowl of fresh blackberries covered with Devonshire cream—or, really, a bowl of practically anything covered with Devonshire cream. I wouldn't be surprised to find her pouring Devonshire cream on eggplant or steak-and-kidney pie or matzo brei.

After Alice had absorbed a couple of dozen truffles and a gallon or two of Devonshire cream, I felt I might be able to take her to an Indian restaurant without having my *paratha* spoiled by thoughts that she was about to cause a nasty scene. On previous trips to London, we had been taken to Indian dinners by a friend whose commitment to organizations working against the discrimination that exists toward immigrants from the Indian subcontinent and the Caribbean has been, I always assumed, a shrewd device for acquiring inside information on Indian restaurants. Our host at Alice's first post-truffle Indian meal was another friend with what I took to be a similarly selfish devotion to bettering race relations in Great Britain. Confident that he had at last found an Indian restaurant that would please Alice, he dismissed our previous guide as a specalist in the problems facing Jamaicans and Trinidadians—a man whose inside information did not extend past codfish and yams.

"Well, what did you think?" he asked Alice, after we had finally finished an elaborate five-course meal.

"The best Indian food I ever had," Alice said with a shudder.

"What do you suggest we eat in the place of Indian food?" I asked Alice the next day. I had just finished a very satisfying English breakfast of eggs and sausages and grilled tomatoes and kippers, but I had that anxious feeling I get sometimes in parts of the American South when, after finishing a fine Southern breakfast of eggs and grits and little country-sausage patties made into sandwiches with biscuits, I realize that the high point of the day may have passed before nine in the morning.

"Natural food in England is extraordinarily good," Alice said.

"You know health food disagrees with me," I said.

"Natural food is not the same as health food."

"It certainly isn't in my case," I said. "Unless long-term nausea is your idea of health." If one of her attacks of diet balancing had come over her, I told Alice, she could comfort herself with the reminder that the filling in one English sausage probably satisfies the minimum daily cereal requirement for six months.

I resolved to redouble my efforts to find decent pub food in London, or maybe a fish-and-chips café that actually fried the fish when it was ordered instead of in a mass fry-in with all of the other fish at six in the morning. The closest fish-and-chips café of quality that I knew about was in Brighton. Several people had recommended as the best fish-and-chips restaurant in London a place that was noted for the length of its wine list—a place I naturally dismissed out of hand, the way I would dismiss a barbecue joint in Arkansas that also served lobster tails and chow mein. The pasties at the pubs I had been eating at in London tasted like meat and veggies cleverly repackaged in a crust hard enough to be of some use if the pub happened to be the sort of place where the patrons tend to start throwing things at each other late in the evening. Whenever hunger overcame me at a pub, I had taken to ordering a Ploughman's Lunch—basically cheese and a roll and chutney—on the theory that its ingredients at least remained immune from attack by the man in the kitchen. I found eating Ploughman's for that reason depressingly reminiscent of a defensive gin-rummy player I once knew whose strategy was based on ridding himself of all high cards as quickly as possible and was expressed in the motto "Lose less."

But was I ready for health food? Aside from the fact that it has always seemed bad for my health, what would people say? Most of my eating discussions are, after all, with the kind of people who could be categorized roughly as Big Hungry Boys—people who offer to let me in on the supreme tacito joint in East Los Angeles if, in return, I promise to keep the information to myself and to search my mind for suggestions as to how someone with a strong pastrami habit can survive in Cheyenne, Wyoming. What would Fats Goldberg, the pizza baron, someone who believes that green vegetables should be consumed only by small furry animals, say if I answered his inevitable question about eating in England by telling him I hung around health-food shops, gulping down wheat berries and bean sprouts? Could I really discuss whole-grain bread with chili heads and knish freaks?

"Let's just stop in to see what they have," Alice said one day, as we passed a health-food store called Sesame, near Primrose Hill Park. "Maybe we can have a picnic in the park."

I hesitated. I was famished. Alice had suggested that if I didn't take a meal or two break from Chinese food I might start nodding off from monosodium glutamate. We were a long way from Brighton. I was a bit embarrassed about going back to the fish-and-chips place there anyway: on our previous visit I had, under some pressure from Alice, removed some of the batter from my fish, making me feel like a pudgy secretary who had saved a few calories by removing the top slice of bread from her chicken-salad sandwich at lunch. I glanced quickly up and down the street to make certain that Fats Goldberg was not lingering nearby. Then we went in.

I had to admit that the salad did not produce immediate queasiness. The quiche was a great improvement on those leaded Frisbees that have been delivered to us now and then in Stuff-Stuff with Heavy joints through the efforts of two strong men and a reinforced handcart. What seemed truly remarkable, though, was the pizza. Natural-food pizza! It was actually pizza ingredients—tomatoes instead of tomato sauce, for instance—spread on top of heavy, whole-grain bread and toasted under the grill, the way your mother used to toast the ham-and-cheese sandwich for you at lunch if you had behaved yourself all morning.

"You don't seem to be having any difficulty eating the pizza," Alice said.

"The dissolution of the British Empire is complete when what you buy in health-food stores tastes better than real food," I said.

"I think it's all marvelous," Alice said.

"Maybe we should head over to Golder's Green," I said. "I feel O.K. so far, but it would ease my mind to be close at hand to an antidote. Just in case."

By the time we got back to England again, I had reason to be optimistic about what we would find there to eat. Charlie Plum, our foreign-correspondent friend, had been on the job in London for several months, and I assumed he had made a small hobby out of checking out fish-and-chip joints. I had been informed by some other specialists in the field that a new fish-and-chips café on Lisson Grove was causing lines around the block. A flash memory of a Singapore noodle dish we had once eaten at Chuen Chung Ku, on Wardour Street, had inspired me to write Plum about investigating some of the Singapore restaurants that had opened in London. I phoned Plum as soon as we arrived. He said that I might like to have lunch at Sweetings, a plain fish house in the City, but his suggestions for the serious dinners we had planned were virtually all French restaurants.

I was astounded. "Could he have become a connoisseur

of Stuff-Stuff with Heavy?" I asked Alice. "Who would have thought it of a man who travels with Arthur Bryant's barbecue sauce?"

What seemed to disturb Alice the most about my conversation with Plum was the news that in an effort to find the perfect dining spot he had eaten in sixty French restaurants in London within a few months. (When Plum's friends are asked to name his principal charms, they often mention relentlessness.) Alice feared that eating in that many London French restaurants in such a short time could lead to someone's entire system going into heavy-cream arrest.

The restaurant we decided on—a French seafood place in Chelsea called Le Suquet—did not appear to be in the Stuff-Stuff with Heavy tradition. The atmosphere was informal. The proprietors were obviously French people instead of one of those English couples who seem to use up a considerable part of their energies making certain they have the correct pronunciation of Bourguignon. Any suspicion I had that appearances might be decieving—that a trout stuffed with a shrimp stuffed with an olive stuffed with a pimento was about to appear, submerged in white cream sauce à la Elmer's—was swept away by the appearance of a startling assortment of shellfish. There were mussels and clams and oysters and langoustines and crawfish—all of them giving every indication of recent experience in salt water.

"You must admit . . ." Alice said after a while, her voice emerging and then fading away from behind a teetering pile of empty shells.

"I suppose the debates all those years about whether or not to join the Common Market weren't meaningless after all," I said, as soon as I disentangled myself from a crab claw. "This is what they must have meant by 'entering Europe.'"

The meal at Le Suquet was very much in Alice's mind a couple of weeks later, when we returned to London from visiting the Jowells in Somerset and had only one meal left before returning home. Although we had made our usual trip to Golder's Green—tradition must be observed—I still felt the need of more fried seaweed. I had not been able to find time for the fish-and-chips place that was said to be stopping traffic on Lisson Grove, and I still wanted to check out the Singapore places, which Plum had failed to investigate in his obsessive pursuit of the best French restaurant in London.

All of which does not explain how I found myself sitting across the table from Alice at a small French restaurant called Ma Cuisine—the other French restaurant Plum had enthusiastically recommended.

"You're doing this all for me," Alice said.

"It's nothing, really," I said, trying to remember precisely the expression Humphrey Bogart used when he arranged to have Ingrid Bergman fly off with Paul Henreid while he remained to face the Nazis with Claude Rains. "I'm sure I'll get some fish and chips someday. Probably."

The first course arrived. I had ordered red mullet soup. I tasted it. It was staggering. It was so good it immediately joined a sort of soup pantheon that sloshes around in the back of my mind—Gladee's chowder, for instance, and the gumbo we ate at the andouille gumbo cook-off sponsored by the Jaycees in Laplace, Louisiana, and some lentil soup Alice once made with a stock based on the carcass of a smoked turkey someone had sent us from Greenberg's in Tyler, Texas.

"This is really sweet of you," Alice said. "Considering

how much you really like all of that disgusting fish and chips."

I shrugged modestly as I ate. It occurred to me that the line outside of the fish-and-chips place on Lisson Grove might not mean anything anyway, since English people like standing in line so much they often just queue up as a way to pass the time.

"It's very nice of you to come here just because I wanted to," Alice said.

"It's nothing," I said. "Really."

IO

A Softball, a Lump

I once became acquainted with the plight of three young lawyers in Omaha who were painfully conscious of the city's limitation as a gastronomic capital—all of them having at one time or another tasted the delights of Kansas City.

"It's as if somebody prepared for the French foreign service in Paris or Lyons and then got assigned to Liverpool for the duration," I explained to Alice.

"Mmmm," Alice said. "Could you please pass the sour cream?"

Alice and I were having our discussion just after I had received a letter from one of the lawyers, a Creighton University law professor named Michael Fenner, informing me that he and his two colleagues at the bar had discovered the greatest steak house in the world—a place that served sirloin steaks he described as "the shape of a softball, only bigger."

"I better get on out there," I said to Alice. "Those young fellows are suffering, and somebody has to give them some encouragement."

"What makes you think they're suffering?" Alice asked. "He says right in the letter that they've discovered the best steakhouse in the world. It also says that he likes the food in Omaha, that Omaha has the best cheeseburger in the world, and that there are several other eating experiences in Omaha nobody should miss."

"Midwesterners are noted for making the best of any situation, Alice," I said. "I thought you knew that by now."

I understood how the attorneys in question were suffering. The one generalization that it may be safe to make about lawyers—except, of course, for the statistically incontrovertible one that this country has quite a few more of them than it has any need for—is that the profession includes a large number of serious eaters. Once, when some employees of a noted steakhouse in Washington were arrested on narcotics charges, the waiters involved found themselves with immediate legal aid from attorneys who had represented some of the most prominent Watergate figures, and the maître d' showed up in court with a partner in the firm headed by Edward Bennett Williams. One of the three Omaha lawyers, a hefty young man named Daniel Morisseau, who works for the Union Pacific Railroad, has about him such a palpable interest in food that, I later learned, a taxi driver who once took him and some other travelers from the Memphis airport to downtown hotels pointed out governmental and cultural sights to the passengers in general, then slowed down at a corner, looked straight at Morisseau, and indicated the entrance to the city's premier barbecue establishment.

In the rather informal survey I have taken over the years on intensity of interest in food by profession, lawyers rank only a few trades below concert pianists, who are as a group undoubtedly the most devout searchers-out of quality restaurants—a phenomenon I can account for only with the theory that concert pianists, who travel constantly, quickly come to realize that the alternative to finding a decent place to eat on their own is having dinner at the home of the chairman of the local Philharmonic's hospitality committee. Reporters rank pretty low in my survey, partly because of the curse they share with the Irish. I once ate regularly with the members of an American newsmagazine bureau in Paris who had the custom of eating lunch as a group every Saturday, and the restaurant they favored always turned out to have been chosen for the perfection of its dry martinis. Once they found a bartender who had mastered the art, they tended to follow him from restaurant to restaurant, the way a group of concert pianists would follow a gifted but temperamental sauce chef.

Once I had met the three lawyers in question, I realized I had been quite right about the extent of their misery in Omaha. None of the three had grown up there—they were raised and educated in various parts of Missouri and Kansas—so when they talked about restaurants with the sort of nostalgia that can sometimes make up for whatever the sauce lacked, they were talking about restaurants in some other city. The nostalgia did not seem to be associated with restaurants of their childhoods. Michael Fenner, who grew up in St. Joseph, Missouri, recalls having practically no interest in eating until he happened to go to law school in Kansas City—where he met Dan Morisseau, and where, judging from their reminiscences, the two of them must have had to pick out the words in their contract texts through the barbecue-sauce stains. Fenner also spent a few years in Washington, working for the Justice Department, and he shared quite a few meals there with John E. Smith, a lawyer from Atchison, Kansas, not far down the Missouri River from St. Jo, who was then working for Senator Dole and later became the house attorney of an Omaha trucking company. Fenner still likes to talk to Smith about eating in Washington—the Cuban food at the Omega and the Middle Eastern food at the Calvert Cafe and the chili at Hazel's Texas Chili Parlor. Fenner believes that Hazel's recipe was so secret that she carried it with her to the grave, although some other Washington eaters believe that it was handed down intact to a man with a tattoo, and still others believe that it was not the sort of recipe anyone would have to guard very closely. Fenner's favorite restaurant in the Washington area was the renowned Silver Spring fish house called the Crisfield Seafood Restaurant. He misses practically everything about Crisfield's.

"They know how to treat children," I heard him say once.

"They know how to treat oysters," said Morisseau, who did some eating in Washington himself.

The exchange came in the midst of one of the discussions the three lawyers have had about how the food in Omaha compares with the food in other cities they have lived in. They do all seem to like Omaha, and they have been adventurous about seeking out the food of ethnic groups that an Easterner might not expect to find in Nebraska—Mexicans, for instance, and Bohemians. But Morisseau, after some careful research, concluded that what passes for barbecue in Omaha is just beef covered with a mixture of ketchup,

Tabasco sauce and a concoction called liquid smoke. Fenner decided that Italian food in Omaha amounts to pouring red sauce over whatever happens to be on the plate —a Midwestern Italian variation of the way Alice uses Devonshire cream in England. A couple of years after Morisseau moved to Omaha, he made a trip to New York, and he had trouble shaking his astonishment at rediscovering that there are Italian restaurants without red sauce and Chinese restaurants without chow mein. For someone who has accommodated himself to the limited number of restaurants in a Midwestern city, the quantity as well as quality of New York restaurants can be staggering. About the time Morisseau made his trip, someone published a book that dealt only with the Chinese restaurants of New York; it was two hundred and sixteen pages long, the authors having decided to limit themselves to eighty restaurants out of what the Chinatown Chamber of Commerce estimated to be about one thousand.

"We gave up a lot of food when we came here," one of the lawyers said during the discussion. "What we got was steak."

Omaha, of course, has a few dozen steakhouses—typical Midwestern red-meat palaces except that, the proprietorship being almost universally Italian, the customary side dish is spaghetti rather than hash browns. But the steakhouse Fenner had mentioned, a place called Dreisbach's, is in Grand Island, Nebraska—a hundred and forty miles away.

Fenner and Smith and Morisseau had most recently eaten at Dreisbach's on the way to a law seminar in Kearney, Nebraska, but when I informed them that I was coming to Nebraska to cheer them up, they seemed untroubled about just driving out to Grand Island from Omaha for dinner. Morisseau—the only one of the three who might qualify in some circles as an Easterner, having been raised in Kirkwood, Missouri, near St. Louis—has a fondness for the West that encompasses pioneer history and Western railroads and driving across the flat reaches of Nebraska which have caused many other travelers to sum up the state as being "just too far across." Smith and Fenner once drove an hour and a half to Peru, Nebraska, to eat dinner in a restaurant called Peru Seasons. (They liked it, but the proprietors decided to move to Costa Rica.) The trip to Peru was an activity of an informal eating club that they and their wives and four other couples belong to. Every month or so the women of the club cook a special dinner out of a particular cookbook or from the cuisine of a particular country. Twice the club had lobsters flown in from Maine. The men handled one meal, in the summer, and, having traveled to Kansas City for the supplies, they held a sort of taste-off between the barbecue sauce provided by Arthur Bryant's and by Gates Barbecue, a worthy if less legendary competitor.

It is not the sort of club in which a lot of eating time is wasted on talk about the bouquet of the wine or the texture of the crêpes. When it's called anything, it's called the Omaha Gourmands. The most memorable remark made at any of its functions came when one member was finishing up some of the main course directly from the serving platter —an understandable way to pass the postmeal lull, as far as I'm concerned—and another member said, "Please don't eat the spoon." There was some talk of translating that into French and putting it on a club T-shirt. Morisseau is not a member of the club, but he may be even more interested in quantity than the Omaha Gourmands are, particularly when the quantity in question is of beef. Morisseau is what used to be called a "meat and potatoes man"—in his case, a lot of meat and plenty of potatoes. The steak rumor he is most interested in investigating is a tip that the Elks Club in Ogallala, Nebraska, serves a twenty-eight-ounce sirloin.

I had looked upon Fenner's letter not only as an opportunity to buck up the spirits of some exiles but also as an opportunity to try overcoming what I acknowledge is a strong prejudice against eating in steakhouses. It is a prejudice I blame partly on living for too many years in the East, where the atmosphere in most steakhouses is the strongest argument I know for vegetarianism. While the rest of the country is becoming littered with steakhouses that have "themes" like Old Depot or Western Barn, the theme of New York steakhouses remains The Big Shots Meet the Tough Guys. Doormen say "O.K., Mac" as they accept five dollars for parking a customer's Mercedes; waiters say "Yeah, lady" when a female patron asks if she may have the sixteen-dollar filet. The male customers tend to have the look of people who are proud of themselves for having just slipped the headwaiter about what they paid their secretaries that day and for figuring out some way to take it off their taxes. A lot of the female customers are prime specimens for a game Alice and I used to play to pass the time during intermissions at the Broadway theater—trying to guess how long some particularly glossy culture lover in the first eight rows spent dressing for the evening.

Aside from the fact that the atmosphere of most New York steakhouses is a threat to anyone's digestion, I must admit that, unlike many of my countrymen, I do not feel the need of a pound or so of red meat every day or two to stave off the perils of anemia. My mother has often said that I am not a "real steak eater"—real steak eaters being, as I understand the term, people who hold up dessert for a long time while they gnaw on the bones. Alice has occasionally made similar remarks, although rumors that she has taken over my mother's role in cutting up my steak for me are certainly exaggerated.

I have long suspected, I must admit, that a blind taste test would be as embarrassing for the people who go on about the superiority of one steak restaurant or another as it would be for the people who take a blood oath of loyalty to a particular brand of Scotch—or as it already has been for a law professor who boasts about the unique splendor of his eggs. On the other hand, I do like steak. There used to be a steak restaurant on the outskirts of Kansas City I loved going to, but after I heard some rumors that it had switched from charcoal broiling to gas, I decided against returning—partly because R. C.'s fried-chicken restaurant interposed itself between the steak restaurant and town, and partly because I might find it embarrassing to finish off a twelve-ounce filet and still not know for certain whether the rumors were true.

Fenner's letter was, as Alice had said, enthusiastic about the eating opportunities in Omaha. He suggested that I come at least a day early to try some of the local specialties before we drove to Grand Island, although when I arrived he seemed to be strapped about where he and his wife and I should go for lunch. He had heard—incorrectly, as it later turned out—that the obvious place, a stockyards bar that

served Mexican food and was called V. I. P. South, had
closed. He settled on Joe Tess' Place, which specializes in
scored carp. There is no mention of carp on the menu.
Perhaps because the carp has had some difficulty overcoming a reputation as an ugly-looking beast that spends a lot
of time nosing around in the mud, Joe Tess' menu has always identified the specialty merely as Famous Fish. Joe
Tess charges sixty-five cents for a Famous Fish Sandwich,
with an extra ten cents for specifying a rib or tail cut. The
rib cut costs the same as the tail cut; it's the luxury of
making the choice that costs a dime. Apparently, bitter
words are spoken now and then at Joe Tess' Place when a
diner who has paid a dime for specifying ribs finds that his
dining partner got ribs just in the luck of the draw. There is
some controversy about what the best part of a carp is, and
there are a good many people who believe that there isn't
any best part of a carp. Mike Fenner's wife, Anne, sounded
like one of those. The most she could manage to say after
trying her first plate of Famous Fish was, "Well, that's got to
be unique."

Her husband seemed discouraged. "You kind of hate
being from a place that's famous for that," he said.

John Smith told us later that the secret is in the preparation. "In Atchison, you nail the carp to a board and lean it
up against the fire until the board starts to get kind of
black," he said. "Then you turn it over and nail it to the
other side of the board and lean that next to the fire until
that side of the board gets kind of black. Then you eat the
board."

"Well, it's got to be kind of unique," I said, when Alice
asked me on the telephone that night about our lunch.

"How about dinner?" she said. We had eaten dinner at a cheerful Bohemian bar whose proprietors had such a strong Midwestern feeling about not carrying the divisions of squabbling Europe to the New World that they furnished "extra gravy" designed, as far as I could tell, to apply equally to Polish sausages, German sauerbraten, and Hungarian goulash. I told Alice I thought the high point of the meal came when Morisseau responded to a choice of two vegetables by saying, "I'll take double dumplings—that other stuff grows under the ground."

"Is there a French restaurant there you could try?" Alice asked.

"A what!" Alice was perfectly aware of my having stated in public print that a good French restaurant would come to Omaha about the time decent barbecue hit the Paris suburbs. I was willing to admit that the French restaurants in London had been a pleasant surprise, but Great Britain happens to be a bona fide member of the European Economic Community. For years I have gone around the United States assuming that good food is available if the careful traveler sticks to regional specialties and the cooking of ethnic groups strong enough to have at least two aldermen.

"Don't forget about André's," Alice said. André's is a French bakery in Kansas City that I have never entered. For years I brushed off suggestions that I go there by saying that someone who had only a few days in town to get down what might be several months' supply of superior barbecue and fried chicken had no time for such frivolities as finding out what the western Missouri version of a brioche might taste like. Then, in 1976, Mimi Sheraton, the redoubtable food critic of *The New York Times*, wrote an article informing Republicans who were about to travel to Kansas

City for their national convention that André's had croissants better than any she had ever been able to find in New York. Alice, it almost goes without saying, adores croissants.

"André's was a fluke, Alice," I said. "Like a magnificent potato latke in London. A Traveling Person has to play the percentages." According to the percentages, a fancy French restaurant in Omaha was likely to be long on menu descriptions and short on taste. On the other hand, Alice and I had missed a lot of croissants playing the percentages in Kansas City. Could I have been wrong all of those years? How bad could, say, trout amandine in a Midwestern French restaurant be? I shuddered, having just remembered.

Omaha, of course, does have a fancy French restaurant. The next day, just out of curiosity, I asked Morisseau what it was like. He dismissed it as not serving steak "except for the fancy kind."

"Good point," I said, regaining my confidence. I was ready to push on to Fenner's cheeseburger joint.

According to the plan the three lawyers had devised, we were stopping at Stella's Tavern, a hamburger place near the S. A. C. air base, to stoke up for the drive to Grand Island. Morisseau arrived at Stella's with some random train talk he apparently considers appropriate to the beginning of any journey ("The Ford FAST's running on time. The ARRO's five minutes late. Trains are speeding the nation's vital resources to their destination so that American consumers can consume everything that can be scratched out of the ground") and some words for Smith's benefit on the trucking industry ("Will the slaughter on our highways never stop? Is there no end to the carnage wrought by the Killer Trucks?") Stella's served up, as Fenner had predicted, a quality cheeseburger. It was not Kansas City quality, perhaps, but certainly nothing that would force any-body back into nostalgia for a Cuban restaurant in Wash-ington. The cheeseburgers were accompanied by red beer—beer that has been mixed, for reasons that defy the imagination, with tomato juice. Smith remarked that the red beer served some years before at Sellen's Pool Hall, in Russell, Kansas, was better than Stella's, and I think he must have been right. Everyone was looking forward to the journey, although for long drives Morisseau prefers the stark plains of western Nebraska to the central part of the state, where he has been heard to complain, "There are trees blocking the view."

I asked about the steak served at Dreisbach's, thereby launching my companions into what I believe lawyers call a colloquy:

"It's like a softball—sort of round."

"No, more like a lump."

"I'd prefer to say 'round' rather than 'like a lump.' "

All of the attorneys were willing to stipulate that the tenderness of Dreisbach's steak was beyond question. Fen-ner had written me that Dreisbach's furnished knives only on the chance that some diner might want to slice up the skin of his baked potato.

"My mother often says I'm not a real steak eater," I said as we waited for our steaks at Dreisbach's. No colloquy followed. My dinner companions exchanged what I inter-preted to be wary glances. Dreisbach's was full, even though it was only about six. We had found ourselves arriv-ing an hour and a half ahead of schedule, despite a stop at a café in Wahoo whose chocolate-chip cookies Smith admires and a tour of the Stuhr Museum of the Prairie Pioneer and a slowdown to practically a dead stop at every railway crossing so that Smith could demonstrate to Morisseau the difficulty any innocent citizen out for a drive has in crossing the Union Pacific tracks without breaking an axle. Dreisbach's had turned out to be a huge, windowless brick restaurant hidden in a string of franchise joints along a double lane just on the edge of Grand Island. A plaque in the lobby indicated an Award of Excellence for Bread and Rolls from the Wheat Division of the State Department of Agriculture. I was put off a bit by a subheading under "Soups" on the menu that said "Heinz Individual," but I was cheered by the sight of the other people in the dining room—mostly families, with a pleasant absence of either Big Shots or Tough Guys.

The steak did look like something between a softball and a lump. I rather enjoyed it, even though the waitress had acknowledged that it had been broiled with gas, not charcoal.

"Well," I said to the attorneys as I finished the last of it. "I've tasted worse steaks."

"That is not exactly the response we were looking for," Morisseau said.

"Your trouble is that Omaha is not Kansas City," I said.

"Omaha's not a lot of places," Fenner said, taking on a wistful, Crisfield's sort of expression.

"Well," Morisseau said, "at least you can come out here and eat steak without having someone shove cold spaghetti under your nose." Midwesterners are noted for making the best of any situation.

A couple of months after my trip I got a letter from some people who identified themselves as members of the Omaha Wine and Food Society. They had heard about my visit.

They said that had I merely visited the appropriate *haute cuisine* palaces my "tastebuds would have rather roamed among classic foods of excellence." That sounded enough like the sort of menu those *haute cuisine* palaces have to confirm my belief that I had been wise not to sample what I believe the international gourmets categorize as Cornhusker French.

I also received another letter from Mike Fenner. "Omaha has a Korean restaurant which we kept from you the first trip, and a place that serves excellent pan-fried chicken," he wrote. "There is also a wonderful place on the banks of an otherwise undeveloped stretch of the Missouri River. One can sit outside and eat catfish (much better than carp) or fried chicken (deep fat, I suppose) while watching the river roll by . . . There is plenty to come back for."

"They sound desperate," I said to Alice.

"I suppose you think the only honorable course is for you to go back and try to buck them up," Alice said.

I thought about my meals in Omaha for a while. "No," I finally said. "I think the biggest help I can be to those young fellows is to encourage them to get by on their own resources."

II

Goldberg as Artifact

I was not surprised when I heard that the Smithsonian Institution had expressed an interest in the neon sign on Fats Goldberg's pizza parlor. I have always thought of Fats himself as an American artifact, although he is ordinarily regarded as a medical wonder rather than a piece of straight Americana. What has brought doctors around to the pizza parlor now and then to have a stare at Fats and poke him around a bit is not merely that he once lost some one hundred and sixty pounds—no trivial matter in itself, being a weight equivalent to all of Rocky Graziano in his prime—but that he has succeeded for nearly twenty years in not gaining them back. Apparently, keeping off a large weight loss is a phenomenon about as common in American medicine as an impoverished dermatologist. Because Fats is now

exceptionally skinny, most people call him Larry instead of
Fats. Nobody, as far as I know, has ever called him Mr.
Goldberg. Alice and Abigail both call him Larry; Sarah,
who likes to keep him distinguished in her mind from another friend of ours named Larry, has always referred to
him as Larry Fats Goldberg the One Who Makes Pizza. I
still call him Fats. Having known him in Kansas City long
before he let his Graziano slip away from him, I have difficulty thinking of him as anything but a fatty. He has even
more difficulty than I do. He is, he cheerfully admits, as
obsessed with food now as he ever was. (Fats cheerfully
admits everything, which is one reason nobody has ever
thought of calling him Mr. Goldberg.) Convinced that remaining a stick figure is the only alternative to becoming a
second mountain of flesh, Fats has sentenced himself to a
permanent diet broken only by his semiannual eating binges
in Kansas City and, during the rest of the year, a system of
treats on Mondays and Thursdays which reminds many
New Yorkers of alternate-side-of-the-street parking regulations. His semiannual eating binges are so gargantuan and
so infectious that Alice makes a small hobby out of seeing
to it that Fats and I are never in Kansas City at the same
time.

After six or eight years in the business, Fats became
rather restless with the life of a pizza baron. "You can't
schlepp pizzas all your life," he often told me. He began
phoning regularly for our reaction to the schemes he
thought up for new lines of work. What Fats's schemes have
always had in common is that they are invariably concerned
with food and they are invariably among the worst ideas in
the history of commerce. At some point, I reluctantly came
to the conclusion that Fats may be like one of those nov-

elists whom publishers speak of as having only one book in them. It occurred to me that, as far as moneymaking business schemes go, creating the brilliant bi-ethnic concept of Goldberg's Pizzeria might have just done Fats in.

Sometimes Fats seems to prefer discussing his schemes with Alice instead of me—perhaps because he is aware that people in Kansas City sometimes refer to her, in respectful tones, as a "gourmet cook." It is certainly not because she is more encouraging than I am about the commercial prospects of, say, an edible diet book or a pizza cone. In fact, I at least mentioned to Fats that a better name for Goldberg's Pizza Cone might be Goldberg's Pizza Cohen, before telling him that it was, by whatever name, one of the truly dreadful ideas of the decade. When Alice answers the telephone, says "Hi, Larry," and then says something like "That is just awful—one of your absolute worst," I know that the Larry she is talking to is Larry Fats Goldberg the One Who Makes Pizza. As far as I know, Abigail is the only person who has ever taken any of Goldberg's ideas seriously. When he began to talk a lot about an invention of his called a pizza pusher—a hard-plastic instrument that would allow someone to eat a piece of hot pizza without burning his fingers— she asked him about its progress every time she saw him. "I'd really like to try it," she always said. Abigail has actually eaten a trial version of a pizza cone—pizza dough rolled into the shape of a cone and then filled with what more pedestrian operators put on the top. "It's very good, Larry," she said. "It really is." Fats beamed.

I don't know how to account for Abigail's sympathy for the Goldberg schemes. It is true that when we go to Goldberg's Pizzeria on Sunday evenings Fats always lets Abigail make her own pizza; it is true that he occasionally shows up at our house carrying a heart-shaped pizza for Abigail, her initials done up in green pepper. But he has always performed those same services for Sarah, and the noise Sarah made when she saw the pizza cone defies any attempt at reproduction. My own response to ideas by Fats has been fairly consistent. When I hear about something like a scheme to produce an edible diet book, I usually say, "Fat Person, there are worse things than schlepping pizza."

Fats mentioned the Smithsonian accession during one of our Sunday evening visits to the pizzeria. Having had some time to reflect on it, he told us he was not at all surprised that a place like the Smithsonian Institution wanted his sign. "It was a nice piece of neon work," he said. As it happened, one of the regular customers at Goldberg's Pizzeria works for Chermayeff & Geismar Associates, the firm commissioned to design a five-year Bicentennial exhibit for the Smithsonian called "A Nation of Nations." When the customer suggested that Goldberg's sign might be suitable for a display that would amount to a selection of ethnic neon, Fats said, as he later remembered it, "You want me to take it down now or will you come back for it?" (A Smithsonian curator came back for it, Fats having in the meantime ordered a precise replica to take its place.) Fats's cooperation was based partly on an understandable pride ("There I'd be with Lucky Lindy and everybody") and partly on a quick calculation of how many pizza eaters might pass through the exhibit in five years.

It is natural for a restaurant proprietor to see publicity as a way of attracting customers, but Fats has probably been alone among his peers as seeing it also as a way of attracting a wife. Ever since his emaciation, in his mid-twenties, Fats has thought about finding an appropriate wife almost as much as he has thought about food, and he tends to regard publicity as a sort of singles ad. In the days when Alice thought Fats was serious about finding a wife, she used to spend some time trying to persuade him that his search should be less dependent on such devices as striking up conversations on Madison Avenue buses. Eventually, Alice decided that Fats did not genuinely want to get married, even if he found someone who, in addition to meeting all of his other requirements, was willing to commit herself to a lifetime of semiannual eating binges in Kansas City. I still try to help by suggesting that some of his requirements are unreasonable—a requirement, for instance, that the prospect not be seeing a psychiatrist. I have tried to explain to Fats that among young women of certain backgrounds in New York seeing a psychiatrist is merely a ritual of the culture, like foot-binding once was among young women of certain backgrounds in China. Fats remains unconvinced. He thinks that anyone who sees a psychiatrist is "a little twitchy." Also, he says that when he thinks of his intended telling all to some psychiatrist, he himself feels "a little twitchy."

Fats has often been mentioned in the press—in articles about pizza or about men's fashions (his views on clothing are as deeply rooted in the fifties as his views on courtship and marriage; sartorially, he is best known for an addiction to saddle shoes) or about what celebrated New Yorkers like to do on Saturdays in the city ("Larry Goldberg, a bachelor who operates Goldberg's Pizzeria on 53rd Street and Second Avenue, said he spent his Saturdays at Bloomingdale's, where he rides the escalators and 'looks for girls' "). Somehow, though, Fats could never get over the fear that there were still a few people in New York who had never heard of Goldberg's Pizzeria. So in his travels around town he continued to spread the word by handing out small paper Goldberg's menus that list pizzas with names like "Moody Mushrooms" and "Bouncy Meatballs" and "SMOG" (sausage, mushrooms, onions, and green peppers)—the last a house specialty that Fats has described on the menu as "a gourmet tap dance." Extracting a menu from Fats has never required strenuous persuasion. "I don't press them into the hands of accident victims, or anything," Fats once told me. "But I did hand them out to the orchestra at Radio City Music Hall one night as they came out of the pit after the last show."

I thought I ought to go to the opening of "A Nation of Nations" with Fats; he was, after all, the only person I knew from whom the Smithsonian Institution had ever collected anything. Alice thought the trip was a good idea as long as Fats and I did not find it expedient to travel from New York to Washington by way of Kansas City. Fats has never been seriously tempted to break his regimen by the food of any other city. I have always found the food in Washington what might be expected of a city dominated by people who are willing to put up with the gray meat and spongy chicken of political dinners year after year merely for a seat in the Senate.

Fats was looking forward to the opening as his first trip to a museum in the role of a benefactor. He is not one of those New Yorkers who never seem to take advantage of the city's great museums. He long ago decided that museums are ideal places to strike up a conversation with someone who just might turn out to be the future Mrs. Fats Goldberg.

"On Sundays I schlepp through Central Park and stop

for a rest on the steps of the Metropolitan," he once told us. "But I never go inside. The Metropolitan depresses me."

"You mean because of all those Egyptian tombs and everything?" I asked.

"No, it's mainly families," he said. "For girls the Whitney's the ticket. I usually work the Whitney on Sunday afternoons. I used to go in, but now I just work the lobby and save the buck and a half."

The subject of museums had come up suddenly, as I remember, during a conversation at our house about a business scheme Fats had concocted—a plan to offer a sort of food tour of New York that would take visitors from one ethnic delicacy to another for four or five hours.

"Fats," I said. "I hate to be the agent of your disillusionment once again, but I think you should know that many people do not customarily eat for four or five hours at a stretch. Many people eat breakfast and wait a few hours before eating lunch. Then they go about their business for a while, and then they eat dinner."

"Three meals a day!" said Alice, like some zealot who is always lying in wait for the opportunity to get a plug in for one wacky cause or the other.

Fats looked puzzled. When he is not on a diet—that is, when he is in Kansas City—he does not exactly divide his eating into meals, even if he does continue to use phrases like "then on the way to lunch I stopped at Kresge's for a chili dog."

For several months he stopped talking about his ethnic-food tour and concentrated on the edible diet book, which many connoisseurs of Goldberg schemes believe to be his worst idea ever. "Don't you see it?" he would say. "The whole thing would be edible. Food coloring for ink. I haven't figured out what we could use for the paper, except maybe pressed lettuce, but we'll find something. Can't you just see Johnny Carson eating one on television! Each page would have menus for the three meals of the day, but one of the meals would be the page—so, for instance, you'd just eat that page for breakfast."

"If you ate the page for breakfast, Fats, how would you know what to eat for lunch and dinner?"

"It'd sell like crazy," Fats said, ignoring my quibble. "Bloomingdale's, Neiman-Marcus, Marshall Fields. *Goldberg's Edible Diet Book*. I'd autograph them at the cookbook counter at Bloomie's. I hang around there a lot on Saturdays anyway. The cookbook counter is the best place in the store to meet girls."

On the flight to Washington for the opening of "A Nation of Nations," I asked Fats if I was about to witness the first visit he had ever made to a museum for any purpose other than to look for girls.

"Who said I won't be looking for girls tonight?" Fats answered. He is a man of strong habits. He acknowledged that he had a thick wad of paper menus in his suitcase. "If there's a flat place in front of the sign, I might just spread some out fan style," he said. "It might be very artistic."

For the rest of the flight, Fats talked about some of his business ideas—including a sort of singles restaurant that would feature Fats as an auctioneer ("If only I could figure out what to auction, it would be a natural"), and a Sunday-morning catering service called Brunch à la Goldberg, and a lecture tour as the Thin Evangelist. The concept of the Thin Evangelist evolved, through a mutation or two, from an evangelical fat lady named Sister Sara Lee, who was the main character in a skit performed by the monumentally unsuccessful comedy team of Berkowitz and Goldberg— one of the Fat Man's pre-pizza parlor schemes. It is central to the Thin Evangelist act that Fats begin each lecture by stepping out from behind an air-filled plastic reproduction of himself as he looked when he weighed three hundred and twenty pounds, and he told me he had been concerned about the problem of the Goldberg balloon springing leaks during all the traveling necessary for the lecture circuit. Having heard some of the lines from the Sister Sara Lee routine, I was prepared to tell Fats that his problems with the Thin Evangelist act probably went beyond leakage, but he suddenly seemed to lose interest in the lecture circuit in his enthusiasm to explain the commercial possibilities of his plastic pizza pusher. He seemed particularly proud that it had only one moving part.

Fats had dressed carefully for the opening. He was wearing a faded blue Western shirt with the collar spread back to display a V of white T-shirt, peach-colored Levi trousers, a Madras sports jacket, and a pair of black-and-white Spalding saddle shoes with authentic red rubber soles—a type of saddle shoe apparently as rare and difficult to replace as a 1947 DeSoto. Fats said he keeps the Spaldings secreted in the back of his closet in their original box, to be taken out only on special occasions. Having read in the press releases that "A Nation of Nations" would include not only Thomas Jefferson's desk and George Washington's mess kit but also an original ticket booth from the 1923 Yankee Stadium and a selection of American comic books, I felt obligated to warn Fats that an overzealous curator might well snatch the saddle shoes from his feet and install them in a display case between a pair of 1919 spats and a Dacron Nehru jacket, circa 1968. "Keep both feet on the ground, Fat Person," I said.

We had dinner at a Georgetown fish house—a place that has on some occasions shown indications of being within fish-hauling distance of Chesapeake Bay and on another occasion raised the possibility in Alice's mind that the necks that had once been attached to the soft clam bellies served by Gage & Tollner were not being donated to the *Times* Hundred Neediest Cases after all. Fats ate very little—not because he was nervous about the opening but because it was neither Monday nor Thursday. At the Smithsonian he shifted from foot to foot while the opening ceremonies were going on. Then, the moment they had ended, he walked through the door of the main hall and strode purposefully toward the neon-sign display—not bothering to waste a glance at the Indian artifacts or the display of political buttons or the reconstruction of a 1940 Fort Belvoir enlisted men's barracks. Suddenly he was standing before an array of neon. A smile spread across his face. He looked prouder than I had seen him look since the time Abigail told him that his ethnic-food tour sounded like a lot of fun. The GOLDBERG'S PIZZERIA sign was in a central position, high above IRISH ROSE BAR-GRILL and WARSAW FOOT LONG. A discreetly designed caption said, "Goldberg's Pizzeria, 996 2nd Avenue. New York City. Designed by Fred Stenger. About 1971." Fats hesitated for a moment. Then he pulled some menus out of his Madras sports jacket and put them on a broad railing in front of the signs. A few minutes later, while Fats was at the other end of the display, grumbling about how much space had been given to huge McDonald's signs in foreign languages, an elegantly dressed man walked up to the railing, picked up some menus, and said to his companions, "I can't believe it—Larry Goldberg was already here." Spotting Fats, he said, "Don't you ever stop?" Then he started laughing.

"That was the guy from Chermayeff and Geismar," Fats said later. "He's a small anchovy."

"Is that like a Big Enchilada?" I asked.

"No, no," Fats said. "He has a small anchovy pizza when he comes in for lunch."

Fats seemed impressed by the exhibit ("Terrific, from start to finish") but disappointed by the crowd. He shook his head sadly as we left. "The Whitney's the ticket," he said.

"Did I ever tell you my idea for a fat belt?" Fats said as we sat on the plane back to New York.

"I'm sure you haven't," I said. "It sounds like the kind of thing I would have remembered. Maybe that was one you tried out on Alice."

"It would say 'You Are Fat' on the outside, and there would be a calorie counter on the inside," Fats said. "A little gimmick. You know—a little show business."

"I don't believe you should try that one out even on Abigail," I said. "I think that idea might be even worse than the edible diet book."

"I don't know why you say that," Fats said. "I've received nothing but huzzahs since I've discussed it with anybody. Peggy thought it was the best idea in the world."

"Peggy who?"

"Peggy Owens, my haircutter," Fats said. "She cuts my

hair for three large SMOGs and three heart-shaped SMOGS."

"She sounds like an astute woman, Fats," I said. "But I'm not sure a talent for barter transfers well into modern merchandising. Also, I'm not sure why we're discussing such things when you should be telling me about your feelings on this historic occasion. Were you proud and humble last night?"

"I was proud and humble, and I thought it was a giggle," Fats said. "That a pizza schlepper would be there with all the biggies!"

Not long after the opening of "A Nation of Nations," Fats informed us that he had sold the pizza parlor—transforming himself into a pizza baron emeritus.

"I hope this wasn't based on any assumptions about hitting it rich with the pizza cone, Fat Person," I said. "I feel I should tell you that if Abigail said anything about having her finger on a lot of venture capital, she was talking through her hat."

"It's my greatest invention," he said. "We're just having a little trouble working out the right dough. My baker is getting a little twitchy."

Sarah and Abigail were also concerned about how Fats was going to support himself—and whether their Sunday kitchen privileges at Goldberg's Pizzeria were over. Fats assured us that he would still be at the pizza parlor in the role of consultant to the new owners. He said he even had a supply of free pizzas. The contract calls for Fats to receive one large SMOG a day—total of said SMOGs to be cumulative. We were there a few weeks later, and Fats presented

Abigail with what he insisted on calling a "prototype" of the pizza pusher. Abigail lost a slice or two trying to eat with it, but that did not seem to affect her opinion of its usefulness. "It's a very good invention, Larry," she said. "Really."

12

Air Freight

When Alice and I were walking through the American Pavilion at Expo '76 in Spokane, gazing at a pile of mangled appliances displayed as just one example of the crimes we had all been guilty of perpetrating against the environment, I thought I recognized a refrigerator that had been displayed spanking new in the Argentine Pavilion at the Brussels World's Fair in 1958. At that time, it was presumably being displayed to offer silent rebuttal to anyone who might have ever considered the notion that Argentina was incapable of cooling its own loin steaks. I don't feel responsible for solid-wasting refrigerators myself. Even if I did, I wouldn't be enthusiastic about paying admission to be reminded of it. I have disposed of no refrigerator since 1958. As it happens, though, almost superhuman restraint —the sort of restraint that many people, some of them in my own family, do not believe I possess—was required to avoid destroying the refrigerator we now own when the first and only breakdown in its history caused the spoiling of some crawfish *étouffée* I had just lugged all the way from Lafayette, Louisiana, under twenty pounds of dry ice. To this day, whenever I hear some environmentalist go on about modern man's tragic dependence on electricity, I think of my spoiled crawfish.

I don't mean to leave the impression that I always return from a trip with something for the freezer. The country ham I got in Horse Cave from the Chaneys, for instance, was stored on top of my filing cabinet, Boots Chaney having assured me that it could be left out "for a year or two." The freezer, though, is often full. I have always operated on the assumption that being, say, within a couple of hours of Santa Fe and not dropping in to get some tamales from Mrs. Lina Rivera goes against the American belief in the value of enterprise shown and opportunities seized.

I came across Mrs. Rivera's tamales during a difficult period, when I was trying to gather some regional delicacies for a party that would demonstrate to some New Yorkers the sort of food they were being deprived of daily. There were enough complications to leave me with a permanent admiration for the patience of museum curators who put together shows by borrowing masterpieces from a variety of institutions and private collectors. First, I phoned the only man in southwestern Louisiana who had the facilities to airmail crawfish pies to New York, and he told me I had neglected to write him a thank-you note two years before, after he took me out in his boat on the Atchafalaya Basin. It took a day and a half to compose a letter of apology to him that Alice thought struck the right balance between abjectness and obsequiousness. Then Pat Uhlmann, a friend of ours from Kansas City, said that he would be willing to fly to New York on the day of the party with the necessary supply of Arthur Bryant's ribs, but only if we would refer to him in all correspondence as "Bearer of the Ribs, Keeper of the Sauce." Knowing Uhlmann to be a man of his word who merely happens to have some unusual ambitions—he once concocted a scheme, gracefully vetoed by his wife, to buy his birthplace and turn it into a national shrine—I finally agreed.

Then I discovered that the tamale supplier I had hoped to use for the party, a friend of ours who lives in Arroyo Seco, New Mexico, had turned her attention away from tamale-making in the direction of goat-raising. I was forced to telephone another friend in New Mexico, a psychiatrist in Albuquerque named Bob Bergman, who had no special credentials in the field of tamales. I did know Bergman to be an eater of considerable scope. He had just finished several years as chief of the mental health programs of the Indian Health Service—based in Window Rock, Arizona, on the Navajo Reservation—and he seemed to have visited just about every restaurant in the country that is anywhere near any Indians. I suspect he has eaten at Dreisbach's more often than the lawyers from Omaha have. Being a pilot of some experience, he often made his rounds in a small private plane—a fact I have tried not to hold against him, even though the impression I always have while circling over LaGuardia in a commercial airliner that has been told to wait an hour for a runway is that dozens of private planes must be clogging the landing pattern, touching down with their loads of corporation executives and rock stars and political candidates and other people who would probably be doing everybody concerned a favor if they stayed home in the first place. Bergman just happened into Grand Island, Nebraska, one night when he had to make a stop between Aberdeen, South Dakota, and Plainview, Texas, and found the hospitality there extraordinary; it included literally being met by a red carpet, and being chauffeured to Dreisbach's and back by the motel manager. He then started stopping off whenever he was in the area. Sooner or later, he realized that other private pilots were doing the same thing. I told him that I thought all private pilots should fly to Grand Island, Nebraska, and stay there.

Bergman, acknowledging a lack of expertise in the field, agreed to search out a Spanish-speaking tamale specialist who would know for certain how to find the best green-corn tamales in New Mexico. A few days later he called to inform me that I might be looking for blue-corn tamales, since green and blue are the same word in Navajo. I began to worry that I had chosen the wrong tamale man.

"I didn't ask for a scholarly footnote," I told him. "I need tamales."

Bergman called the next week with a more encouraging report. A Spanish-speaking colleague named Gil Duran, who was from Santa Fe, had given him some serious assurances about the work of Lina Rivera. Duran had even volunteered to drive to Santa Fe with Bergman for the pickup. When I came through Albuquerque a couple of weeks later, Bergman handed over two sealed pasteboard boxes of tamales, packed in dry ice.

I tried to appear appreciative, but my concern about the tamales, which I had not tasted or even seen, must have been strong enough to communicate itself to a man in Berman's line of work. "Don't worry—I'm sure they're great," he said. "Gil wanted to eat a couple of them on the way back from Santa Fe even though they were frozen solid." My trust proved well placed, of course. As it turned out, Lina Rivera is to tamales what Yonah Shimmel is to knishes.

The realization that my own trips need not be our only source of freezer treasures came to me one day when Fats Goldberg was about to fly off to Kansas City for one of his eating binges. He asked me if he could do anything for me while he was there—doubtless thinking that he was only making a polite gesture.

"Yes, Fat Person, as a matter of fact, there is," I said. "You can go to Arthur Bryant's barbecue restaurant and pick me up three pounds of spareribs, not forgetting a few handfuls of burnt edges, and then you can bring them back to New York and heat them up slowly in your pizza oven and watch me eat them—that's what you can do for me."

Since then Fats has a standing order from me. Once the ribs are safely in the freezer, I telephone the family that has been chosen to share the celebratory meal—the family having been chosen on the basis of strong Kansas City credentials or several years of extraordinary behavior. I have always assumed that my call touches off unrestrained joy throughout the fortunate household, although once, when the phone was answered by the strictly vegetarian roommate of a friend who had been selected, I was reduced to saying, "Just tell Henry the goods from Kansas City have arrived."

The arrangement has failed to work only once, when Fats returned from Kansas City bearing ribs but informing me that the burnt edges—the burnt edges of barbecued brisket which are presumably why both the Democrats and the Republicans held conventions in Kansas City within two years—had inadvertently been left in his mother's freezer.

"Are you telling me that your dear old mother in Kansas City stole my burnt edges?" I asked the Fat One.

"No, I just forgot them," Fats said.

"I certainly wouldn't have thought it of her," I said. "After all these years."

"She didn't do it," Fats said. "She doesn't even eat barbecue."

"I wouldn't have thought that of her, either," I said. "She always seemed very nice."

"Quit talking to Larry that way," Alice said. "They were just some burnt edges. It's not that important."

"I'm sorry, Fat Man," I said, trying to work up a smile for Fats and a glare for Alice. "I got excited."

Not that important! Why would Alice make a remark like that? Could it be, I began to wonder, that she had what one of Bob Bergman's colleagues might call a repressed hostility toward my attempts, as an old-fashioned American breadwinner, to assure my family a full larder against the possibility of drought or siege? Not long after the burnt-edges incident, Alice made still another suspicious remark. I was about to leave for LaGuardia Airport. Bergman happened to be on his way from Albuquerque to upstate New York, and had offered to hand over some tamales between planes.

"Must you really do this?" she asked me.

"I'd hate to think of poor old Bergman moping around LaGuardia all that time by himself, without even anybody to talk to," I said. "I think he may have as long as twenty-five minutes between planes."

"That's not why you're going," Alice said.

"He's also carrying chili verde," I admitted.

"I don't know why you've gotten yourself into this thing," Alice said.

It suddenly occurred to me that Alice may have overheard me say "The goods from Kansas City have arrived" on the telephone and misunderstood the sort of substance I was dealing in. I tried to reassure her. "Don't worry," I said. "Green-corn tamales have been de-criminalized."

Alice's real concern about the tamale drop was based, of course, on the suspicion that I would not start on the six-week raw-carrot torture she had devised for me if the freezer was filled with ribs, tamales, chili verde, Aunt Sadie's blintzes, and a number of other targets of opportunity. She has no strong moral feelings against tamales. On the other hand, the country ham I had acquired in Horse Cave through the good offices of the Chaneys had been drawing what I interpreted as disapproving glances from Alice for a few months whenever she happened to pass by my filing cabinet.

"If you're concerned about its appearance," I finally said, "I want you to know that Boots Chaney assures me the newspaper sticking to it is an authentic detail, like a piece of grit on a very expensive free-range egg." Kentucky is full of stories about sophisticates from the East ordering their first country ham, then throwing it away when it arrives because its appearance leads them to believe that a disaster has overtaken it in the mails. Although I tried to explain to Alice that the ham looked the way it was supposed to look, I also tried to face the fact that I was married to someone who had grown up in Westchester County, New York, blithely extracting the hearts from artichokes.

As it turned out, though, what Alice distrusted about the

ham was the recipe Tom Chaney had typed for me. At first, I thought the stationery he used—with its legend about widows being tended and whiskey being hauled and lies being told—had given her the false impression that the Chaneys were not serious people when it came to ham. Alice was not bothered by the stationery. What bothered her was that Chaney's recipe, which called for baking the ham in a sort of crust that was then disposed of, said that only three hours and twenty minutes were required in the oven.

"According to what it says in James Beard, it should take about ten hours," Alice said.

"James Beard!" I said. "James Beard puts squid in his chili!"

James Beard, however worthy he may be in every other respect, does put squid in his chili. I am privy to this fact from having attended what must be described as an international chili confrontation in Manhattan at the home of a Hungarian gourmet. It is true that I find discussions about what properly belongs in chili to be on the same level of interest as detailed descriptions of new wonder diets or explanations of how to outperform the market, but I believe it would be fair to say that putting squid in chili is not what people in Kentucky would refer to as Down Home.

"I'm not going to have anything to do with fixing this ham," Alice said. At that moment, I remembered her commenting at the chili confrontation that she found the idea of squid in chili "very imaginative."

"I'll fix the ham," I said. I found an assistant, of course. In the kitchen, I'm mainly an idea man, although I did have Abigail complimenting me on my Cheerios until she wised up at about the age of three. First, I phoned Tom Chaney, who sounded rather hurt when I asked him if the recipe could possibly be dangerous. "That has been the best country ham recipe in Kentucky since the mind of man runneth not to the contrary," he said. "If you're worried, you could use a meat thermometer, I suppose, although I would naturally never use no such a thing."

"Who shall we have over to eat the ham?" I asked Alice, after the meat-thermometer compromise seemed to give some assurance that guests would at least be safe.

"How about Bill and Genny?" Alice said.

It was not a suggestion that showed a lot of confidence in my ham. Genny Smith is a kindly person who would probably compliment the president of McDonald's on his Big Mac rather than hurt his feelings. Her husband, Bill, is widely known as the Man with the Naugahyde Palate. His standards of cuisine were set, rather rigidly, at the Bob's Big Boy outlet in Glendale, California, and he would not know a country ham from a parking meter.

My assistant and I began our task—scrubbing off several back issues of the Hart County *Herald*, and preparing the crust in precisely the manner directed by the Chaney family recipe. We put it in the oven and attached the meat thermometer. In exactly three hours and twenty minutes, the thermometer showed precisely the correct temperature for a ham that is ready to be eaten.

"Maybe the Beard recipe allowed for having the ham covered with truffles or pâté de foie gras or something," I told Alice.

My assistant removed the crust, and we served the ham. It was magnificent. Even Alice was dazzled.

"It's always nice to see you, Bill," I said to the Man with

the Naugahyde Palate. "But I'm sort of sorry we didn't invite James Beard."

A few weeks later, I happened to be passing through Horse Cave, and I was able to report the triumph personally to Tom Chaney—repeating it a few hours later for Boots Chaney, and giving a shortened version to Aunt Daisie Carter.

"Tom says no hard feelings about the country ham," I told Alice on the telephone that night. "He's sending you a gift."

"How nice," she said. "What is it?"

"The local Cheddar," I said. "It's kind of a funny color, but Tom says you'll love it."

13
The Sound of Eating

At least I'll know what to say if a marriage counselor ever asks whether we have one subject that seems to provoke tension in our marriage again and again. "New Orleans," I will say. "Eating in New Orleans, counselor."

"Do you mean that the Chez Helène Incident was not an isolated incident?" the marriage counselor will say.

"Hardly," I will reply, as Alice sits without comment in the corner, stuffing herself with Prestat truffles covered with Devonshire cream.

"Would you like to talk about it?"

"Nothing would give me more pleasure," I will say. "Except perhaps eating in New Orleans, which nobody around here ever seems to let me do in peace." I will then present, in a calm and detached way, what the marriage counselor will come to know as the Jazz Festival Incident.

We had just decided to take in the New Orleans Jazz & Heritage Festival one spring when Alice said, "It would be a great time to visit some of those lovely plantation houses along the river."

I have nothing against plantation houses. I have gone without complaint once or twice to a plantation house outside New Orleans that has been made into a restaurant serving a passable copy of the baked oyster dish whose original inspired me to suggest that a statue be erected in Jackson Square of the inventor—Mrs. Lila Mosca, of Mosca's roadhouse, in Waggaman, Louisiana. (My proposal calls for the statue to be carved out of fresh garlic.) I had to face the possibility, though, that Alice might be talking about visiting plantation houses that served no food whatsoever. Part of marriage, after all, is trying to protect one's husband or wife from potential weaknesses or excesses, and it occurred to me that Alice was in danger of developing an unhealthy interest in exteriors.

"How can you decide to go to a jazz festival in New Orleans, the birthplace of jazz, and then talk about spending any of your time staring at a bunch of façades?" I asked Alice.

"Are you claiming that you're going there to listen to jazz?" she asked.

"Well," I said, confidently. I didn't think I should go any further than that. I do like jazz. I particularly like the sort of New Orleans street jazz heard at, say, a funeral held for a member of the Eagle Eye Benevolent Mutual Association or a Founder's Day Parade staged by the Jolly Bunch Social Aid & Pleasure Club—the sort of jazz nobody can hear without falling in behind the band and half-dancing down the street in a movement New Orleans people call "second-lining." I like the way jazz can be used in New Orleans to make what could be an ordinary event special. In fact, I once hired a jazz band to meet Alice as she arrived at the New Orleans airport from New York—a gesture, I might feel compelled to tell any marriage counselor, that was not made under the assumption that she would start talking about plantation houses or diet plans the moment she got off the plane. In fact, the jazz festival happened to be going on during the weekend I hired the band—although we were able to stop in only briefly, having a previously made engagement at the Crawfish Festival in Breaux Bridge. There was some difficulty finding a band that was free at the time Alice's airplane was scheduled to arrive, I remember, and a friend who was acting as what I suppose would be described as my band broker said, "How would you feel about having foreigners?"

"You mean from Houma or Morgan City or someplace like that?"

What my band broker meant, it turned out, was a band made up of musicians from abroad who had come to New Orleans for the festival. There has always been a strong interest in New Orleans jazz in Europe and Japan; in the late fifties, when not many white people in New Orleans itself seemed very interested in New Orleans music, it used to be said that no jazz funeral was complete without a body, a band of music, and two Englishmen. The band that broke into "Hello Dolly" as Alice came down the ramp was led by a London antiques dealer who played trumpet as if he had grown up on Toulouse Street. I was not surprised. I have always believed that New Orleans jazz can be exported; it's the oyster loaves that won't travel.

Whatever my interest in jazz, though, it was true that my

interest in attending the New Orleans Jazz & Heritage Festival had been aroused when a New Orleans friend of ours named Allan Jaffe told me what was available at the festival food booths. According to Jaffe, the eating side of the festival had developed over the years in a way that might make it possible for a jazz fan to eat jambalaya from Gonzales just a few steps from the booth where he had eaten andouille gumbo from Laplace on the way to eat boiled crawfish from Breaux Bridge.

My conversation with Jaffe had taken place over some baked oysters, cracked crab salad, barbecued shrimp, spaghetti Bordelaise, and chicken Grande at Mosca's—Jaffe and his wife, Sandy, having whisked me to that Louisiana Italian shrine from the airport one evening after I had figured out that a traveler who truly wanted to get stuck between planes in New Orleans on the way from Mobile to New York could arrange it. Jaffe is thought of by most people in New Orleans as the manager of Preservation Hall, a jazz hall that was an important element of the New Orleans jazz revival in the early sixties, but he thinks of himself as a tuba player. He certainly has the sort of appetite that might be associated with a tuba player. Before Buster Holmes retired, Alice felt pretty much the same way about my going to Buster's restaurant on Burgundy Street with Jaffe as she did about my going to Kansas City with Fats Goldberg—although, as far as I can remember, none of the meals I ate at Buster's with Jaffe lasted more than four or five hours. Jaffe, who was raised in Pennsylvania, is not shy about eating outside of Louisiana—when he is traveling with the Preservation Hall band, he is apparently quite gifted at devising reasons for detours that take the bus past Pat's, the cheese-steak emporium in South Philadelphia, or past Arthur Bryant's Barbecue—but, given his appetite for New Orleans food, he has been struck on the road with cravings so desperate that Buster has to rush to his side by first available jet, laden with red beans and rice. "As much as I eat in New Orleans, though, I've only gained about five pounds a year since I came here," Jaffe told me in the late sixties. "The only trouble is that I've been here nine years."

"Could it be that Allan Jaffe mentioned something about the food at the jazz festival that night you stopped to eat at Mosca's on the way back from Mobile?" Alice asked.

That is what I mean by suspicious questions. I can't imagine what led Alice to believe that Jaffe and I talked about the jazz-festival at that dinner; as I remember, I reported to her at the time that our conversation had consisted mainly of speculation on whether or not Mrs. Mosca maintained her own garlic ranch hidden away somewhere in St. Bernard Parish. (Alice had raised the subject of garlic herself the morning after I arrived home from my Mosca's layover: she had not heard me when I crept quietly into the bedroom at two or three in the morning, she said, but while stirring in her sleep sometime before dawn, she had gathered from the presence of a strange odor that a wild beast had somehow found its way into the room.)

Confronted with the truth about my conversation with Jaffe, I told Alice that eating all sorts of Louisiana specialties at the festival instead of having to drive all over the state to find them should appeal to any citizen eager to do his or her part in conserving our country's limited supply of fossil fuel.

"To you a jazz festival is just eating with background music," Alice said.

"Jazz and *heritage* festival," I reminded her. "It's called

The New Orleans Jazz & Heritage Festival. And what do you think the heritage of New Orleans is—macramé? In New Orleans, heritage means eating."

"With so much going on at the Fairgrounds, one has to be fairly well prepared ahead of time to catch as many good acts as possible on a given day," I read in *The Courier*, a New Orleans weekly, after we got into our hotel room. "This year there are five stages, three smaller gazebos (labeled A-C), a jazz tent, and a gospel tent." I could see the problem. In the eight years since we had stopped briefly at the jazz festival on our way to Breaux Bridge to eat crawfish (or, really, on our way to Opelousas to eat roast duck and dirty rice on our way to Breaux Bridge to eat crawfish), the festival had grown from a two-day event held at a local square to a huge undertaking that covered the Fairgrounds Race Track with people for two three-day weekends in a row. Since we had come for the second weekend, we had the opportunity to prepare ourselves by telephoning a New Orleans friend named Gail Lewis for whatever tips she could offer from having attended the first round. "The crawfish is expensive but good," Gail told me. "There's O.K. red beans and rice. Stay away from the oyster pie. Also skip the fettucine unless you're nostalgic for your mother's macaroni-and-cheese."

"Gail says the red beans and rice are O.K.," I told Alice. "She didn't try the oyster loaves, so we might have to stop at the Acme to have two or three before we go out, just in case. The ladies from the Second Mount Triumph Missionary Baptist Church have a booth again selling the fried chicken that apparently caused Jaffe to seek salvation last year. I think everything's going to be all right."

Alice was on the other side of the room, looking at an old-fashioned map that decorated the wall. I went over to read the map's inscription. It said, "Plantations on the Mississippi River from Natchez to New Orleans, 1858."

"Don't pay any attention to that map, Alice," I said. "It's nothing but a reproduction."

During another planning session that evening—a planning session held at Mosca's with fourteen of our closest advisers in attendance—I realized that the jazz festival had intensified a problem we always have in New Orleans: we never seem to have time for enough meals. There are simply too many restaurants in town that have been mentioned in sentences that begin, "We can't leave without going to . . ." The problem is serious under the best of circumstances —partly, of course, because of Alice's strange fixation on having only three meals a day—and the necessity of eating for a couple of hours each day at the jazz festival would make it even more acute.

"Anthropologists have found that in many societies four or five meals a day are the norm," I told Alice, halfway through dinner, just after someone at the table had mentioned a smashing soul-food rival to Chez Helène that had been unearthed in Gretna since our previous visit.

"Don't feel you have to keep up with Jaffe tonight," Alice said, ignoring what I thought had been a rather interesting anthropological fact for a layman to have invented. "Remember, he's a tuba player."

The meal was magnificent. After we were through, Jaffe, who had done the ordering, confided to me his suspicion that we had just ordered precisely the same meal for sixteen that we had ordered for three the night he and Sandy had rescued me from the airport.

"There must be some mistake," I said.

"Maybe," Jaffe said. "But tonight I'm not too full."

At some point in its development, the New Orleans Jazz & Heritage Festival turned into the sort of pleasantly unstructured, laissez-faire celebration that Mardi Gras used to be before it absorbed successive body blows from the youth cultures associated with Fort Lauderdale and Woodstock. Some people stand in front of a stage all day, clapping to bluegrass or amen-ing to gospel. Some people stake out a small section of Fairgrounds grass and hold an eight- or nine-hour family picnic, probably listening to nothing much beyond the sound of their own chewing unless one of the marching brass bands happens to wander within earshot. Some people stroll from traditional jazz to Cajun to contemporary jazz, stopping between tents and stages now and then to watch a brass band or some of the brightly dressed high-steppers the jazz festival calls Sceneboosters. Cajun happens to be a type of music I find particularly appealing—partly, I must admit, because for me it carries memories of crawfish, the first good Cajun band I ever heard having been Celbert Cormier and his Musical Kings at the Breaux Bridge Crawfish Festival.

"It's hard to know where to begin," Alice said, when the music started.

"I know what you mean," I said. "There are thirty-two different food booths."

By that time I had already paid my respects to the ladies of the Second Mount Triumph Missionary Baptist Church, whose potato salad turned out to be even better than their chicken, and, not wanting to provoke any schisms among the Baptists, I had also sampled the barbecued chicken being sold by the ladies of the Second True Love Baptist Church. I also felt I should try both versions of jambalaya being offered, and both versions of red beans and rice. Fair is fair.

Three hours after we had arrived at the Fairgrounds I was settled under a tree, almost too full to finish my second hot-sausage po' boy.

"I think you've eaten just about everything that's for sale here," Alice said.

"Not quite," I said. "I refused to eat the avocado-cheese-and-sprout sandwich as a matter of principle. If health food is part of the heritage around here, so is the polka."

"I'm beginning to think we're not going to make it out to the plantation houses this trip," Alice said.

"Probably not," I said. "That would mean we wouldn't have time to go to the lakefront for boiled crabs. Of course, if we treated that lakefront crab eating as a snack rather than as a meal, sort of like tea—"

"I suppose we can at least take a drive to the Garden District," Alice said, paying no attention to what I thought was an extremely sensible solution to one of our scheduling problems.

"Good idea," I said. "There's a place in the Irish Channel whose po' boys I want to try—just a taste, not for dinner or anything—and we could cut through the Garden District on the way."

"Do you want to hear some more music first?" Alice asked.

"Let's go to the gospel tent for a while," I said, rising with some difficulty. "I want to pray for a good harvest."

14
Weekends for Two

In my version of a melancholy walk on the waterfront, I find myself walking through a cold Atlantic mist along the docks of some East Coast city, wearing a turned-up trenchcoat, making the best approximation of footsteps echoing on the cobblestones that can be expected from a man wearing crepe-soled shoes, and ducking into a passage that turns out to be the entrance to a gourmet kitchen-supply shop called something like the Wondrous Whisk—where I soberly inspect imported French cherry pitters and antique butter molds and Swedish meat slicers. The melancholy is produced by wondering why someone who cannot cook spends so much of his time in gourmet kitchen-supply shops. (Was the Cuisinart food processor I bought Alice for Christmas really for me? Could that also have been true of the slicer I bought my mother in 1949 after I saw a man at the Missouri State Fair use one to cut a tomato into slices as thin as playing cards and then spread them into a fan shape on the cutting board, like Doc Holliday showing his aces?) There are some people, of course, who find melancholy aspects in the prospect that, at the present rate of brick-exposing and paint-stripping and beam-uncovering, all old warehouses in all port cities will someday be thoroughly renovated as shopping areas that feature gourmet kitchen-supply shops and purveyors of hardwood toys and restaurants with names like the Purple Endive.

When old warehouses and abandoned factories all over the country started being scrubbed up into boutiques, we Traveling People accepted them more or less the way we had accepted the advent of Holiday Inns—at first marveling at their presence, and then grumbling that they all looked alike. The brick exposed in Ghiradelli Square in San Francisco tended to look like the brick exposed in Pioneer Square in Seattle, which had some similarity to the brick exposed in Old Town, Chicago, or Underground Atlanta or Old Sacramento or the River Quay in Kansas City or Larimer Square in Denver or Gas Light Square in St. Louis or the Old Market in Omaha. I still walk through them regularly—the chic ones and the tacky ones, the ones whose buildings do evoke the history of a city and the ones whose buildings seem a comment only on the history of American brick. I find myself with the sort of conflicting impressions that might be expected of someone who has an aversion to names like the Wondrous Whisk and a weakness for the gadgets that stores with names like the Wondrous Whisk have in them.

Sometimes, on my walks, I speculate that this postindustrial society may have in ten or twelve years produced more handmade pottery than was produced by all of the primitive clay-fashioning societies in the history of the world. Sometimes I am grateful that in an era of suburban chain bookstores run like suburban chain shoe stores it seems natural for a place like Portland's restored waterfront to have a children's bookstore whose proprietors have actually read the books they sell. Sometimes I am fearful that my commitment to civil liberties will someday collapse in the face of a proposal that all producers of macramé be jailed without trial. I have already convinced myself that there are no First Amendment problems about a law that would require shopkeepers to refrain from describing animals or vegetables as being colors the animals or vegetables in question do not happen to come in. If someone wanted to name a bar after an elephant, he would simply have to call it the Gray Elephant or the Dun-Colored Elephant. The Blue Strawberry would be out, which is a pity, since Alice and I once had a spectacular meal in a restaurant by that name on the restored waterfront of Portsmouth, New Hampshire.

"Maybe you could make an exception in this one case," Alice said, after finishing a dessert of huge strawberries served with brown sugar for dipping. Alice is always at her most tolerant after dessert.

"A rule's a rule," I said.

I was on a tour of restored shopping areas along the Atlantic Coast, and Alice had joined me in Boston for the weekend—partly because she wanted to see the Quincy Market restoration on the Boston waterfront, but mostly, I had grown to suspect, because she wanted to go to Steve's, an ice-cream parlor in Somerville known not only for its homemade ice cream but also for its policy of "mixing in" ingredients that range from fresh blueberries to chopped up Heath bars.

"Is Steve's Ice Cream what comes into your mind when

you think of Boston?" I had asked Alice. "Most people think of the Boston Common or Old North Church—or maybe Locke-Ober's, which at least has some characteristics of the traditional fish house."

Alice considers ice cream at Steve's to be an appropriate end to any meal eaten in the Boston area—an area that, in her definition, easily encompasses Portsmouth, New Hampshire. She does not except meals that seem to have ended once already with strawberries dipped in brown sugar. Even with the end of the meal decided, though, we ran into difficulty one day around the restored waterfront of Boston figuring out what to do about the beginning and the middle. The restaurants in such neighborhoods always make me wonder how the word gets around. How, for instance, do all local television newscasters, without having an opportunity to see each other on the air, manage to know when to lower their sideburns three-quarters of an inch or narrow their collars an inch and a half so that they can look precisely alike? How do the proprietors of exposed-brick / hanging-plant / butcher-block-table restaurants in New England know what is being served in exposed-brick / hanging-plant / butcher-block-table restaurants in Seattle? They don't seem to be the type who attend industry conventions. Did the spread of spinach-mushroom-and-bacon salad just happen, or was it engineered by some brilliant agent of the spinach interests trying to pull another Popeye? Who spread the word on putting a celery stalk in a Bloody Mary? Was it the word spreader who told everyone about serving Bloody Marys in goblets? What's his angle? How does everybody know what sort of cheese to have melted on the special bacon-cheeseburger? And which enemy of the language figured out the names? Walking through Quincy Market, we first passed a restaurant called the Magic Pan. Then—after passing a fruit-and-vegetable stand identified by a piece of black-and-white graphic art that appeared to my untutored eye to be a sixteenth-century radish—we came upon a restaurant called the Proud Popover. Then we left Quincy Market and went to Locke-Ober's for lunch. I felt the need to eat at a restaurant named after something that had no astonishing properties whatsoever.

It is customary, of course, for the wives of traveling men to join them for the weekend now and then in pleasant cities like Boston, but ordinarily Alice and I are not among the New Yorkers who are eager to "get away for the weekend." Why would anyone want to get away from a city that has a thousand Chinese restaurants? When we return from Nova Scotia in the fall, the first conversation I fall into about local restaurants often leads me to believe that, far from wanting to spend much time away from the city, I may not even want to leave the neighborhood. The conversation usually takes place in a nearby corner grocery store known locally as Ken & Eve's—a place so friendly that Abigail and Sarah and I would probably use it as our after-school hangout even if it did not have the attraction of old-fashioned gum-ball machines and did not happen to be the exclusive outlet (on a consignment basis) for Keen's Specials, the chocolate-chip cookie to which all other chocolate-chip cookies cannot be compared.

By the time I have my restaurant conversation at Ken & Eve's, I have usually made a quick tour of the neighborhood, just to make certain that everything is as I left it the previous spring. Once, riding my bike down Carmine Street on a crisp fall day, I noticed a sign saying C. & P. SALU-

MERIA ITALIANA over what was supposed to be Frank's Pork Store. I screeched to a halt. Frank's Pork Store had offered one of the true delicacies of the neighborhood—a sandwich of what was called simply "hot cooked salami," made fresh every morning and served warm, with some minced green peppers on top. The sandwich was supposedly "take-out," but I never made it out of the store with one intact. The three men who operated Frank's were always indulgent about someone's wanting to wolf down a take-out sandwich while standing at the counter rather than taking any chances about the salami cooling off. It was always the sort of place where a few bottles of liquor and some paper cups were left on a counter during the Christmas season so that the customers would not be put in the position of offering each other holiday greetings empty-handed.

I parked my bike and raced into the store, shooting a quick glance on the way toward Bleecker Street to make certain that the luncheonette with the remarkable minestrone was still there. At that moment nothing seemed safe. The previous spring, after all, the bakery across Carmine Street that had been, as far as I know, the single source for a type of Italian ring bread made with oregano and lard and cheese and salami had gone out of business—with hardly a murmur from those people in the Village who are always going on about the need to preserve endangered species from extinction.

I burst into the pork store to find behind the counter the same three men who had always been behind the counter. Two of them, it was explained to me, had bought the store from the third—Frank—six years before, and they had finally got around to changing the sign.

"All is not lost!" I said, more dramatically than I had meant to. They looked at me oddly, and to cover my embarrassment, I ordered a hot cooked salami sandwich—extra meat, please, and some green peppers on top.

I then went to Ken & Eve's for the first neighborhood-restaurant conversation of the fall. Like most conversations at Ken & Eve's, it included everybody who happened to be in the store:

"What do you hear about the new Japanese place on Charles?"

"Dynamite! Great sushi. The best soft-shell crabs we've ever eaten."

"You talking about that great new fish place on Hudson?"

"What great new fish place on Hudson?"

"The Danish take-out place with the gravlax and the herring?"

"No, that's on Bleecker."

"On Greenwich?"

"At that new place on Greenwich last night, Eve had a chocolate-mousse crêpe for dessert. Fantastic!"

"Sounds disgusting."

"Chocolate-mousse crêpe! I better get home and tell Alice."

Alice and I, of course, are not completely at a loss for words when we stumble into one of those conversations about the value of married couples picking a favorite weekend spot to dash off to now and then without the children—conversations that have always reminded me of talk-show appearances by the sort of pop psychologist who wears a turtleneck sweater and calls the host by his first name. "Reading," I say when it came my turn to mention our special getaway place.

"Reading, Pennsylvania!" someone always says. Explaining our fondness for Reading is particularly difficult if the group includes one of those people whose tastes run strongly to exquisitely restored country inns with authentic eighteenth-century details and noisy nineteenth-century plumbing.

"You must be joking," the doctrinaire aesthete says. "Isn't Reading just a grimy factory town?"

"Not particularly grimy, as far as I know."

"Is there some sort of country inn near there?"

"There's a motor inn between a cornfield and a shopping center in the suburbs. On the weekends, it has what amounts to a private glassed-in swimming pool. The Sunday *Times* can be reserved at the desk."

"Is there something historic about the buildings? Old row houses or something?'

"Well, there are row houses, but I would say they qualify as historic only in that they give some indication that Reading was once the territory of the single most talented aluminum-awning salesman in the United States."

Alice and I are not actually experts on the architecture of Reading, since we visited the town for some years before we ever saw it in the daytime. We tended to spend most of Saturday in Lancaster County—where Alice likes the quilts and I like the sausages—and head straight for our suburban motel in the evening. On Sunday morning the route we customarily took to the Dutchman's Diner, near Adamstown, happened to bypass the city. At the Dutchman's, the breakfast specials include such local delicacies as country scrapple—cooked crisp, at Alice's instruction, with a poached egg on top—and creamed chipped beef on home fries. The Dutchman's has the added attraction of a twenty-cent surcharge on any breakfast that is ordered after eleven-thirty in the morning—meaning that someone who feels guilty about not getting around to breakfast until the morning church crowd is drifting in for Sunday midday dinner is given the opportunity to pay the wages of sin, but at well below union scale. The only time we spent in Reading itself was on Saturday night, when we had dinner at Joe's—making our way there by a route that permitted me to be sure that one of my favorite American restaurant signs (HOF BRAU CAFE—ITALIAN CUISINE, SEAFOOD) was still in place. Joe's, which specializes in wild mushrooms, does its very best to be a pretentious restaurant—a head-waiter in formal dress, a fancy menu, a room for diners to inspect bottles of the wines available—but the pretension melts away with the first taste of the mushroom soup. I have occasionally mentioned to Alice the possibility of trying a Mao-like running meal in Reading sometime—eating the mushroom soup at Joe's and then dashing across the street to try some of the specialties at Stanley's, which has been identified as "one of the most famous watering holes in Reading" by the authoritative *A Beer Drinker's Guide to the Bars of Reading*, by Suds Kroge and Dregs Donnigan ("Dedicated to our wives"). Alice has always seemed un-enthusiastic about leaving for Stanley's after the soup, and, aware that these weekends are supposed to be special, I haven't made an issue of it.

On Sundays, after our stop at the Dutchman's Diner, we wander through one of the nearby antique markets—Renninger's or Shupps Grove. Shopping is so much a part of any American vacation, of course, that a visitor to Atlantic City strolling along the boardwalk in his swimming suit on an August afternoon is offered several opportunities to buy a fur coat. Our first glimpse of Reading by daylight,

in fact, came because we wanted to observe the phenomenon of thousands of people being bused in from all over the
East Coast to entertain themselves with a day of pure
shopping—Reading having rather suddenly become the
Factory Outlet Capital of the World. "We're really here to
observe," I had to remind Alice as she started to work her
way methodically down a rack of little girls' dresses that
had tiny alligators on them. "It's the phenomenon I thought
you might be interested in."

I don't know whether there is any validity to the theory
that acquisitiveness in America is, like crippling debt, a
natural concomitant of family life and a permanent address,
but it is true that I didn't buy much before I knew Alice. I
worked for a while in Europe when I was young and single,
and when I returned I ran into trouble at customs because I
had nothing to declare. All around me my fellow citizens
were flashing French perfume and Swiss watches and English china. When the customs man asked what I had
bought during a year out of the country and I told him I
couldn't think of anything, he acted as if he might place me
under arrest for Aggravated Prevarication. "Nothing?" he
said incredulously. I tried to conjure up a picture of myself
in some shop buying the specialty of the region, but no shop
appeared. Instead, I kept seeing my draft-board physical
examination, during which an Army sergeant, holding a
form on a clipboard in front of him, had demanded three
identifying marks or scars from a frightened and patently
unblemished young farm boy who was standing next to me.
("I'm awful sorry, sir," the farm boy said, feeling desperately around his palpably smooth chin and searching for
evidence of so much as a freckle on his chalk-white shoul-
der. "Three marks or scars," the sergeant kept saying.)

Finally, I told the customs man I had bought a pair of pants, and he signed my declaration.

I have thought of that scene as I place something like a Victorian hatbox full of Javanese puppets on the counter in front of the customs man and explain that some posters for Abigail's room have been sent ahead—although the dolls both girls are carrying were in fact purchased in England, notwithstanding their similarity to the dolls I bought them in eastern Kentucky to go with the ones I tracked down, in an investigative tour de force, at a small shop in Charleston, South Carolina. The customs man nods, knowing before he asks me that I will be just under the exemption limit. I have been spotted as the type who would have phoned the consulate to make certain that a four-year-old girl is entitled to a hundred-dollar exemption despite her inability to sign her name to a traveler's check. He waves me on—a wise bartender waving good night to a heavy-drinking regular who always manages to stop just before he becomes sick or dangerous. The real answer to the customs man's inquiry about what I have to declare is "A greedy nature, sir."

Still, we rarely buy anything on those Sunday mornings at Renninger's—partly because the prices reflect the fact that there is hardly anything left on the entire continent that is not valued as a part of somebody's collection of something or other. The grotesque lamp base that discourages speculation on what the shade must have looked like turns out to be a find for the collector of "early electrical." Even if we don't buy any of what the voice over the loudspeaker calls "antiques, collectibles and investment items," though, we never leave disappointed. I can always find the funnel-cake stand. Funnel cake is a plateful of twisted dough that has been cooked in oil, covered with powdered sugar, and served piping hot—a regional specialty that some connoisseurs believe to be of about equal harm to the fingers, the clothing, and the stomach lining. Alice, muttering about the grease content as she nibbles on the edges of my funnel cake, always moves in the direction of Pauline Thompson's lunch counter—the only place in the state, as far as I know, that serves coal-black chocolate cake. Mrs. Thompson's cake is the sort of black that in some light looks almost blue. Its origin was apparently in the misdelivery of some dark chocolate to a restaurant Mrs. Thompson once ran—an accident she had the wit to exploit, like an alert chemist who notices that the medicinal substance he has accidentally spilled seems to have a remarkable cleansing effect on the suede of his shoes.

For Alice, dark chocolate is a specialty within a specialty —reminiscent of a collector I once came across at Renninger's who liked all ice-cream scoops but concentrated most of his energies on acquiring the ice-cream scoops that had been manufactured by one particular company. I have heard Alice dismiss elegant and outrageously expensive goodies as "mostly milk chocolate" in a tone of voice rather like the one Francie Jowell uses to say "foreign vegetables."

Alice's feeling of tolerance and well-being after dessert at the Blue Strawberry in Portsmouth is nothing compared to the expansive mood she is in after a piece of Mrs. Thompson's coal-black chocolate cake. She seems so agreeable to any adventure, in fact, that I often find myself ending the weekend with a note of regret—regretting the fact that there are no Indian restaurants within miles of Adamstown, Pennsylvania.

When Alice discovered that the Bonaventure Hotel in Montreal had special weekend rates, I pointed out that the

Bonaventure was bound to lack scrapple, not to speak of the Sunday *Times*. The Bonaventure is run by Western International, one of the more tasteful creators of the new boffo-architecture hotels that permit those traveling salesmen who used to spend evenings on the road sitting numbly in an Esther Williams movie to pass their time staring at the lobby—watching other traveling salesmen ride up and down in glass elevators, or making bets on whether anyone will take a dive from the sixteenth floor of the atrium lobby, or gazing into a half-acre lake that reminds them of the plumbing emergencies their wives are likely to report as soon as they call home.

"The Bonaventure is a lovely hotel," Alice said.

"Western International is weak on costumes," I said. The first time I walked into the Bonaventure lobby I was astonished to find that the bellhops were all Chinese dressed in coolie costumes. I had assumed that there must have been some Chinese phase of Montreal history I didn't know about, but when I went to the Crown Center in Kansas City—a hotel that has, with a rather individualistic vision of environmental protection, preserved part of the hillside it was built on within the lobby—I found the doorman to be an exceedingly tall black man dressed as a Russian folk dancer. The doorman at the Century Plaza, a Western International Hotel in Los Angeles, is dressed as an English Beefeater. I wouldn't be surprised to check in at a Western International Hotel in Nebraska and find that the room clerk is a Puerto Rican dressed as a Southern planter or an Apache done up as a French merchant seaman.

"It has a nicer swimming pool than the one in Reading," Alice said. It is true that the Bonaventure has, in one of its interior courtyards, an outdoor swimming pool that is open year round, but I doubted whether Alice and I would venture into it in January. Steam rises from it in the winter, so that someone observing the action from the lobby is unable to ascertain whether people swimming in ten below zero air are wearing expressions of serenity or intense pain. The temperature of the Reading pool was always approximately that of Lake Lotawana in August.

"Was it the salmon or the Arctic char that was so marvelous at Chez Pauzé the last time we were there?" Alice asked. "It's been so long I've forgotten."

"It has been a long time," I said, reaching for the telephone to call Air Canada.

Once we were in Montreal, of course, I had little time to inspect the Bonaventure's design elements; I was buried in food guides, cramming away like a law school graduate about to take his last shot at the bar exam. I was looking forward to French food, but it had become obvious from all the data that the local cuisine of Quebec was not French but French-Canadian. Eating French food in Montreal is obviously not the equivalent of eating French food in Omaha, but it could be considered parallel to eating Spanish food in El Paso.

"We really ought to have a French-Canadian meal before we leave," I said to Alice.

Alice started thumbing through the food guides. "Well, here's a place that seems to specialize in baked beans in maple syrup," she said. "That must be quite authentic; I can't think of any other reason for serving it."

"There must be other places."

"Yes, here's one that specializes in pig's knuckle stew," she said. "Or maybe you'd like to try one of your Mao meals—pig's knuckle stew here, baked beans in syrup there, then another spot for French-Canadian ham hocks."

"It's always a shame to miss the local specialties," I said, although I was beginning to experience some of the appetite loss I suffered in Martinique when I read Dr. Nègre's description of "a bat worthy of the plate."

"How about that Italian restaurant that was supposed to be so good?" Alice said.

"How can we eat Italian food in a city famed for its own version of French cuisine?" I asked.

"What is New Orleans famous for?"

"It's own version of French cuisine."

"What's your favorite restaurant in New Orleans?"

I paused for reflection, and a school of Mrs. Mosca's barbecued shrimp swam into my mind. (That often happens when I pause for reflection.) "Let's try the Italian place," I said.

We took a taxi to Rue Notre Dame Ouest, a drab street next to the railroad yards, and went into a restaurant called Da Giuseppe. Fifeen minutes later we were eating something called Fettucine Danielle—fettucine with cream and mushrooms and sausages put together in a way that rendered me practically speechless. Marriage, as I have often remarked, is not merely sharing one's fettucine but sharing the burden of finding the fettucine restaurant in the first place. "Alice," I said, as I rolled some fettucine around my fork as quickly as I could roll, "I'm certainly glad you decided to come along."

15
Alice's Treat

When I learned that space limitations would make it impossible for Alice to come with me to a special dinner that was to be prepared in New York by Paul Bocuse, the renowned Lyonnais chef, I secretly resolved to take her to the annual wild-game supper of the United Church of Christ, in Bradford, Vermont. I try to do right by her. Since Alice had spoken for years of wanting to eat a meal prepared by Bocuse, I was determined to make up for the Bocuse bash with a special event she would find particularly appealing— a determination that was not weakened even when she rather overdid her bewilderment at how I happened to have been invited by the publishers of Bocuse's new cookbook to a dinner held for "grown-up food writers." I knew that Alice enjoys church suppers as much as I do. I also knew that she enjoys dishes like prime ribs of beef and steak more than I do—I have always had trouble disassociating such food from testimonial dinners—and I figured that anyone who liked beef was bound to be delighted by buffalo or bear.

When I casually mentioned that the date of the Bradford wild-game supper, an annual event of national renown, was approaching, Alice said, "It's occurred to me lately that it's the idea of church suppers I like more than the food."

"This one is different," I assured her. "Some years they have moose." Then I broke the news: through some strenuous efforts, I had managed to obtain two tickets to the wild-game supper for us. "You can eat French food anytime," I told her. "This is something special."

Alice did not look instantly ecstatic. "Let me get this straight," she said. "Because I won't get to go to a dinner cooked by Paul Bocuse, I get to eat moose in Bradford, Vermont?"

"They don't have moose every year," I said. "I don't want to oversell this."

The Bocuse dinner was held at Lutèce, a distinguished East Side French restaurant that has a custom of leaving prices off all menus except the one given to the host of each party—presumably on the theory that guests should not have to run the risk of having their digestion impaired by the price of the quenelles. We have been taken to dinner there a couple of times by Pat Uhlmann, Bearer of the Ribs, Keeper of the Sauce. As the host of a dinner at Lutèce, Pat has the custom of announcing the price of any dish his guests mention. If Alice says, "I'm thinking about having the *saumon farci en croûte* to start," he'll say something like "A steal at eight dollars and fifty cents." He says it's only fair to give his guests some idea of how warmly they should thank him.

For the Bocuse dinner, I was fortunate enough to be seated next to our friend Colette Rossant, the cook of my dreams, who had translated Bocuse's cookbook from the French. Colette told me that she had taken Bocuse shopping for ingredients in the Village—introducing him to some of the tradesmen she terrorizes daily. They stopped for breakfast at the soda fountain of Bigelow's Pharmacy, a late-morning Village hangout that happens to be only a few hundred feet from Balducci's, the legendary produce store. Bocuse ordered fried eggs, Colette said, and when the counterman asked if he wanted them sunny side up or over, he replied, "As the chef desires."

I was naturally pleased to have Colette at my ear to explain what was going down. It gave me the sort of security I have always felt when Alice is in the seat next to me at a foreign film to let me in on the meaning of the symbolism. (We long ago decided that any foreign film I understood outright can be fairly criticized for heavy-handedness.) Just how fortunate I was to have a specialist nearby was brought home to me after the first course—two pieces of terrine—when Colette said, "I preferred the woodcock to the hare" and somebody down the table said, "Oh my God! You mean they were different?"

Bocuse, wearing an immaculate chef's outfit, was slicing the terrine himself. Although the rest of the meal had been prepared by Bocuse and his assistants in Lutèce's kitchen, he had brought the terrine from France; his method of clearing customs without causing a lot of tiny rules to be quoted had apparently been to choose a customs inspector who looked stout enough to put the matter into perspective.

Bocuse, I was pleased to see, had the build of an understanding customs inspector himself, and seemed to have no sympathy for the low-calorie French cooking that has lately become fashionable. "Without butter, without eggs," he said to his guests, "there is no reason to come to France." I was happy to have some confirmation of my assumption that no sane person would enter one of those French retreats that specialize in three-star diet food without having taken the precaution of strapping a flask of heavy cream to his ankle.

When the fish course was served, Colette told me that *loup en croûte*—or sea bass *en croûte* in our case, since the *loup* does not swim this far from France—was a very old French dish. It occurred to me that I might be able to tell Alice that the fish was nothing particularly novel or unusual. I even thought of asking Colette whether the word "common" could fairly be applied to the dish—until I tasted it. "A very old French dish," Colette repeated. "But this happens to be the best I ever tasted."

Through the rest of the dinner, I found myself trying to concoct uninteresting ways of describing what we were eating to Alice. I could describe the main course as "sort of plain veal," I thought, but could I get away with saying that the macaroni au gratin that accompanied it was done on the same principle as a Kraft dinner? How was I to describe the *oeufs à la neige* that were served between the *fromage de France* ("just some cheese") and *gaufres de grand-mère Bocuse* ("a piece of cake")?

"What was it like?" Alice said sleepily when I finally walked into our bedroom at around twelve-thirty.

"I brought you some chocolate candy," I said. "He gave it out at the end of the meal. I also brought you some cake.

Chocolate cake. *Gaufres de grand-mère Bocuse*, actually."

"Was the dinner any good?"

"Also some cookies. I knew you'd love the cake. I just had a bite or two myself, then I said to the waiter, '*Avez-vous* aluminum foil?' "

"Was the meal any good?"

"Not bad, really. Not too bad."

"What'd you have?"

"Oh, some fish, and meat, and some hard egg-white stuff. You know—that sort of thing."

"Hard egg-white stuff?"

"Did I tell you I brought you some candy? Also some matchbooks."

"They're going to have hare at the United Church of Christ, just like at Lutèce," I told Alice when I phoned her from Bradford the day before she flew up for the dinner. I had gone to Vermont in advance to watch some of the preparations. "It's rabbit pie instead of *terrine de lièvre*, but a bunny's a bunny, right?" I was trying to reassure Alice. Somehow, she had got it into her mind that one of the meats to be served at Bradford was polecat—a misapprehension that I feared was preventing her from viewing the wild-game supper as a class event. "There's no moose this year, but they have moufflon ram instead," I went on. "Not just moufflon ram roast but also moufflon ram loaf. And where else could you get buffalo burgers or bear chops? And no polecat, Alice. I want you to know that nobody around here is even absolutely sure what a polecat is. This is going to be a special event."

"I'm sure it'll be lovely," Alice said, in the voice she sometimes uses to comment on my fourth helping of ribs.

I tried to explain to Alice that the United Church of Christ wild-game supper was the Superbowl of church suppers—out of the class of the kind of church supper she had occasionally referred to as the Annual Starch Festival. Even when it began, in the fall of 1956, it was staged for outside wild-game connoisseurs rather than the local folks —apparently on the sound theory that if a lot of city-bred hunters from Massachusetts were going to swarm into the area every autumn and mow down farm animals while trying to shoot deer, they might as well have a few dollars taken off of them for a good cause before they went home. I told Alice that twelve hundred people were going to be served at the church supper—moving through a buffet line from three in the afternoon until ten at night—and that we were fortunate to be among them, since almost that many had to be turned away. Eris Eastman, the supper's co-chairman, had told me that three young men drove to Bradford all the way from Long Island on the day tickets went on sale at the church, a month before the dinner, simply because they were not willing to trust their luck to the mails. I saw no reason to add Mrs. Eastman's comment that the young men must have been out of their minds.

I also saw no reason to talk to Alice much about the presence on the menu of beaver. Too close to polecat. Marcia Tomlinson—who, along with her husband, Gary, is in charge of cooking for the wild-game supper—told me that there were actually people who came to Bradford every year specifically to eat beaver. "They pass up the pheasant and rice," she said. "They consider that 'restaurant food.'" Apparently, though, a lot of people who are willing to eat most wild game draw the line at beaver—including Mrs. Eastman. ("I'm not sure but what I'm prejudiced," she told me.) There happens to be a theory in Bradford that the game supper was inspired partly by a beaver supper a local man named Richard Shearer used to throw for his pals every year at the Legion hall, but I thought Alice would be more interested in hearing how the supper was founded by Cliff and Helen McLam after they moved to Bradford from East Corinth, where they had run a very successful chicken-pie supper for the Congregational church. "East Corinth is still renowned for its chicken pie," I told Alice on the phone. Alice didn't say anything.

Just before Alice arrived, I bought her a copy of the recipe book the game-supper people had just published. At first glance it seemed rather specialized—the pheasant-and-rice recipe, for instance, yields six hundred portions—but I figured that Alice could make a nice game dinner for two someday merely by dividing all the measurements by three hundred. As far as I could tell from watching the preparation, the Bradford secret for cooking wild game was to subject it to so much soaking in vinegar and water and so much cooking that a diner might have as much difficulty in distinguishing between wild and domestic as some of the visiting hunters always do (in the three days before the game supper, the farm animals that had been felled by gunshots in the area included two horses and a tethered sheep). Aware of the problem of distinguishing between, say, bear sausage and wild boar sausage—particularly when they are crammed on a plate that also contains buffalo, coon, rabbit, moufflon ram, venison, pheasant, and, in some cases, beaver—the church women who pile meat on the plates at the serving line implant in each portion a color-keyed toothpick.

"Aqua is bear," I said to Alice as we finally sat down to

eat. Our plates were piled high with meat—about a pound of meat on each plate, according to Gary Tomlinson's estimate. There were bowls of mashed potatoes and gravy and squash and shredded cabbage on the table. Alice pushed around among the toothpicks for a while. She seemed to be taking very small bites.

"I'm told the venison chops should be eaten as soon as possible," I said. "If they've been off the stove too long the grease congeals."

"Ummm," Alice said, "What'd you say the course after the *loup en croûte* was at Lutèce?" *Quasi de veau bourgeoise* was what she had in mind.

"It was what the French call middle-class veal," I said.

Somewhere down the table somebody said, "I've lost my rabbit livers." It was not easy to keep the various meats separated on the plate, and the toothpicks were not as much help as they might have been if the colors had been more distinctive. I was having some difficulty figuring out where aqua ended and green began. I had already complimented the beaver ("It seems harmless enough") before I realized that what I was eating was marked not with pink but with orange—buffalo. I thought it only fair to remind Alice that at least one of the grown-up food writers at the Bocuse dinner had been unable to distinguish between woodcock and hare.

Alice did not seem to be eating much at all. "The wild boar sausage tastes pretty much like sausage," I said in encouragement.

Alice stared at her plate. Finally, she said, "Could you please pass the squash?"

Fifteen or twenty minutes later, when someone came to clear away our dishes, Alice said, "I notice that you uncharacteristically failed to clean your plate." It was true that I had eight or ten ounces of meat left, although I had probably eaten another four or five ounces in sausages during the day as I watched the preparations. When I had finally figured out which toothpick was pink, I realized that I had spoken too soon about the harmlessness of the beaver. My venison chop had shown some evidence of being fairly long off the stove.

"Well, as you know, I'm not really much of a meat eater," I said.

"While I, on the other hand, have always had this thing about coon pie," Alice said. I gathered from her tone that the Bradford United Church of Christ wild-game supper, an event that seemed to please many diners to the point of seconds and thirds, might have been a disappointment for her.

"I'll make it up to you, Alice," I said. "The Methodist Church in West Fairlee is having a chicken-pie dinner tomorrow, and I'm pretty sure I can get hold of two tickets."

This is certainly not the West Fairlee Methodist Church, I thought to myself, several months later, as Alice and I sat down for dinner at Paul Bocuse's restaurant in Lyons. How someone with nothing more than a simple chicken-pie sort of gesture on his mind happened to end up in France is, oddly enough, rather easy to explain: Alice had just turned forty. (I make that revelation in direct retaliation for her observation some years ago that I had just passed the age limit for joining the Transit Authority Police.) I should make it clear that I did not present Alice with a trip to France as a fortieth-birthday gift. I was simply trying to find a restaurant adequate to the occasion.

Alice is serious about celebrations. Finding a restaurant for even an off-year birthday dinner has always been a problem. She has been consistently unenthusiastic about holding her birthday dinner in Chinatown; she says the restaurants we frequent there are lacking in celebratory atmosphere. I once offered to hold the dinner during Chinese New Year—a period of enormous celebration throughout Chinatown every February—but she declined, on the rather prosaic ground that her birthday happens to be in May. For a few years, Alice seemed pleased with the custom of a long birthday lunch at La Petite Ferme, a tiny restaurant in our neighborhood. Then La Petite Ferme moved uptown, and Alice's response to the notion of trudging up there on a balmy May afternoon was to quote a phrase usually attributed to a traveler in France named Esther Kopkind—*quel schlepp*. Our attempt to have a birthday dinner in some other New York French restaurant expensive enough to mark the occasion ended rather badly at the Box Tree—a small East Side place whose seating arrangements seemed to have been designed by the man who did the IRT uptown local. When our check arrived inside of an early-nineteenth-century book whose pages had been hollowed out to form a little box for that purpose, Alice remarked that some rule ought to prevent restaurant pretension from extending to the destruction of books.

A man who was sitting at the next table—and was therefore just short of toppling into the birthday girl's lap—said, "Are you a librarian?" The waiter informed us, with some disdain, that delivering the check in a hollowed-out book was an authentic custom of seventeenth-century France or sixteenth-century England or some other high-priced civilization—failing to add that their customs also included the flogging of debtors and the medicinal application of leeches.

Knowing that something special would have to be done for Alice's fortieth birthday, I offered to take her to Arthur Bryant's, in Kansas City. She declined, even though I informed her of rumors that Mr. Bryant had recently painted a wall and had acquired a new Royal Crown Cola machine that some customers found quite attractive.

"Well, I guess we better go to Bocuse's place in Lyons then," I said.

Alice looked suspicious. "Are you just feeling guilty about the Bocuse dinner at Lutèce and all that burnt polecat?" she said.

"You know I've never had any guilt of trans-Atlantic magnitude," I said. "I just want to avoid one of those East Side joints."

"You're offering to take me to Paul Bocuse in Lyons because I don't want to have my fortieth-birthday dinner at Arthur Bryant's or Phoenix Garden?"

"Well, that was very good chipped beef on toast you made me on my fortieth, Alice," I said. "And I'm sure if you had known at the time that the chipped beef on English muffin at the coffee shop in the Stanford Court Hotel was even better, you would have arranged for me to be in San Francisco to eat it."

"And you're asking me to go to France just because you think it might be the perfect place for my birthday meal?" Alice asked, still sounding unconvinced.

"Well, to tell you the truth, Alice," I said, "I think I'd like another crack at that *loup en croûte*."

"I accept," Alice said.

"This is only the best thing I've ever eaten." Alice said. She had just swallowed her first bite of Bocuse's foie gras. I was relieved. The previous evening, we had warmed up by having dinner with a friend at another three-star restaurant called Alain Chapel, and I was afraid Alice might have been put off her feed for the entire week by a maître d' so supercilious that he managed to remind everyone at the table of a different despised grade-school teacher.

Alice's appetite seemed fine. She tracked down every morsel of foie gras on her plate, and she seemed to be enjoying the *loup en croûte* even before I reminded her that Colette had praised it as the daddy of all *loups en croûte*. She finished her *volaille de Bresse en chemise*, and her eight or ninety varieties of *chèvre*, and her *gaufres de grand-mère Bocuse*. At Paul Bocuse, Alice is a Clean-Plate Ranger.

"Did it seem O.K.?" I asked.

"Well, I have to say this," Alice said. "I didn't need different colored toothpicks to tell the foie gras from the *loup en croûte*."

I had tried to be attentive to the meal myself after realizing that the truffle soup I ate as a first course could be honorably compared with the andouille gumbo turned out by the Jaycees of Laplace, Louisiana. In fact, my soup pantheon had to be expanded by several gallons in France. A couple of days after the Bocuse dinner, at a sleek hotel in St.-Jean-Cap-Ferrat, I had a fish soup—*soupe de poissons de roche, rouille et croûtons dorés*, to be exact—that was so good I was almost able to forget how much it cost. On our last day in France we realized we might be able to sample a soup that was said to be even more spectacular—a sort of Provençal version of bouillabaisse called *bourride*, which is one of the specialties of a place on the Nice docks called L'Âne Rouge. With careful planning, we figured, we could take a quick tour of the renowned Maeght Foundation museum in St.-Paul-de-Vence, then nip down to L'Âne Rouge more or less on the way to the Nice airport.

The careful planning did not, as it happened, take into account the time required to decide whether the Provençal dolls for Abigail and Sarah ought to be knitting or weaving or carrying a basket of clams or plucking a chicken. By the middle of the morning it was clear that touring the museum would leave us no time for *bourride*.

"It's supposed to be a marvelous museum," Alice said.

"I'm sure it is," I said. "Why else would we have seen six busloads of tourists go in there?"

"There are a lot of Giacomettis," Alice said. She paused. "On the other hand," she went on, "there are a lot of Giacomettis in New York."

"Plenty of Giacomettis," I said.

Alice didn't say anything for a while. She had a thoughtful look on her face. I hoped the thoughts were about the mountain of shellfish she had downed at Le Suquet in London, mixed with thoughts about the sort of seafood a restaurant on the Nice docks might consider worthy of its table. "Let's go to Nice," Alice said.

Did she realize what she was saying? "Well, O.K.," I said. "If that's what you want, Alice, let's eat."

About the Author

CALVIN TRILLIN has traveled the country since 1967 to do a series of articles for *The New Yorker* called "U.S. Journal." He lives in Manhattan with his wife and their two daughters. He is almost always hungry.